On Being Funny

On

Being Funny

Woody Allen and Comedy

by

ERIC LAX

Charterhouse : New York

The author and the publishers gratefully acknowledge the following
for giving permission to quote from the following
copyrighted material:

David Susskind, Talent Associates-Norton Simon, Inc., for excerpts
from the "Open End" transcript of February 14, 1960.
"What's Woody Allen Doing on the Music Page?" by Eric Lax. ©
1973 by The New York Times Company. Reprinted by permission.

The author wishes to thank Larry Gelbart for permission to quote from
the Ingmar Bergman parody as quoted in Chapter 10.

Library of Congress Cataloging in Publication Data

Lax, Eric.
    On being funny.

    Includes index.
    1. Allen, Woody. I. Title.
PN2287.A53L3   791'.092'4   74–25729
ISBN 0–88327–042–0

To my parents

Contents

Photographs follow page 54.

*"My one regret in life is
that I am not someone else."*
—Woody Allen

1.
"Nothing you do here can affect your career in any way."

An October Wednesday in Las Vegas. It has been cold and windy and nasty on the desert all day, unusual for even this time of year. There is nothing to do outside. It is too cold to swim, too windy for tennis or golf. There is no place to walk to except other places to gamble. A stroll is depressing; nothing but cheap motels, gaudy hotels, gas stations (FREE ASPIRIN AND DIRECTIONS!), and wedding parlors with car rental offices in the back. The people on the street, what few there are, are from out of a Fellini movie. A woman, her hair white on the left and black on the right, looks as though a skunk is sitting on her head.

The 1972 National Sash and Door Jobbers convention takes up half of Caesar's Palace, by far the least garish hotel in this neon oasis dedicated to greed and bad taste. The conventioneers, come for some sun as well as gambling, are a little unhappy, having flown all the way from

1

Nashville and Cleveland and Syracuse to weather worse than what they left behind. It is a big day for check-ins and people are lined eight and ten deep at the room clerks' windows, nearly spilling onto the huge casino floor which fills up most of the first level of the hotel.

There are roulette tables and blackjack tables and craps tables in the circular main area; off to one side is a huge slot machine arena and an almost equally huge keno lounge, and on the other side is an area for bacarrat, with a bar beside that. There is a cashier's booth by the craps tables and a hallway that leads to the coffee shop ("The Noshorium") and the clothing and gift shops that feature fifty-dollar cashmere sweaters and clear plastic toilet seats laminated with coins of every denomination.

Across the hallway from the cashier's office is the ticket office for the Circus Maximus, a 1,200-seat restaurant-theater where the headliners play twice each night; the tab is fifteen dollars for dinner and the show. A glass-doored display box, like one for coming attractions at a theater, has pictures in it of Harry Belafonte and Woody Allen.

By late afternoon the conventioneers have all arrived and the hotel is full. The tables are doing a brisk business. Waitresses keep the free drinks coming to gamblers, which is not to say most of them are drunk. Some of them are just stupid, like the pert Nashville girl at one blackjack table who has come to the convention with her parents. The basics, not to mention the subtleties, of the game escape her. She loses the money she brought to gamble with for four days before her stool is warm. Others do better. One man, a high roller who wants to go over the five-hundred-dollar betting limit on craps, has arranged

2

for a table to himself. He sits at the end, his right arm in the pit, his face a bit flushed, while a young girl, maybe his daughter, watches nervously. The four pit men working the table do their job impassively and in silence. He bets between $1,500 and $3,000 on every roll. In twenty minutes he has won $28,000 and quits.

Upstairs Woody Allen is working on three new one-act plays in a suite overlooking the fountains and the gigantic marquee with his and Belafonte's names on it. The view, through latticed bricks reminiscent of a turquoise-cement Persian mosque, has all the awesome splendor one might expect from looking through brick at neon. Little about Las Vegas is subtle—certainly not the salaries of the talent. Woody, working on a contract signed in 1965, will make $85,000, but some performers pull down a quarter of a million for a two-week stand, and a few make more. Others, like Sammy Davis, Jr., and Buddy Hackett, own parts of the hotels they play. Las Vegas is a brightly lit Get Out of Jail Free card.

"Nothing you do here can affect your career in any way," Woody says before going down for the first show at eight o'clock. He is doing Las Vegas for the two simplest reasons: He owes Caesar's Palace one more engagement on his old contract and he hasn't made any money for a year even though he has made two films in ten months. (He will get ten percent of the gross of *Play It Again, Sam*, which means more than one million dollars for him, and he has twenty percent of the profits on *Everything You Always Wanted to Know About Sex*," which will be another million-plus dollars for him, but none of that money will come in for a year or more, and all of it will not come in for years. Filming for *Sleeper* begins in the spring. So

3

he is doing what he has not done since 1968—a stand-up tour of six cities.

In Chicago the week before he played to reasonably full houses, audiences of 2,000 or more. Good, but not what, say, Bill Cosby can draw. In Las Vegas he and Belafonte are filling the Circus Maximus every night. Belafonte is the top name on the bill, so it is Woody who goes on first each show, doing the comic's job of warming up the audience. (He is second on the bill only because this is the one time he has free. Belafonte has already been booked to be the top name and Woody doesn't mind being second. In fact, he likes it, because the responsibility of drawing crowds is on the top name, and "because billing makes absolutely no difference.") Woody could not care less at this point whether he headlines in Vegas or not. He's there to give a good performance, collect his money, and get on with *Sleeper*. He is not at all nervous before going on. Sitting in his dressing room, which is decorated in wild purples and brilliant greens like some mad Henri Rousseau painting, he does a couple of card tricks and talks about trying to catch Milton Berle's show while he's in town.

"I find Berle hysterically funny. He's one of the few people I've gone to see in years. There is a certain kind of broadness one associates with television show presentations like the old 'Milton Berle Show,' as opposed to, say, a much tighter kind of thing like Nichols and May or Sid Caesar. Caesar does a sketch about a Japanese movie, it looks like a Japanese movie. It's very realistic and consequently it's funny. Milton belongs to that school of comedy that's very broad, and of course he's the best of that school. If he does a Japanese movie he comes in with

4

the two teeth hanging down and it's hysterical, but for Milton exclusively. Most of the TV shows had all the stupid broadness of the Berle show without the genius that Milton had. At least when Milton's in women's clothes he's hysterical. He's a guy whose delight in dressing up in women's clothes and blacking teeth out is so spectacular that you're overwhelmed by it."

In the Circus Maximus the audience is pretty well through the meal and fairly high from the drinks and wine. The back of the hall is plushly padded, tiered booths; the floor has long tables. At eight o'clock the lights go down and a voice announces, "Ladies and gentlemen, Woody Allen!" There is warm applause and Woody, wearing a pair of brown and white saddle shoes, corduroy trousers, a blue shirt with a button-down collar open at the neck, and a dark brown checked tweed coat (which anyone with a mind for such minutiae would remember from the film of *Play It Again, Sam*) quickly walks onstage waving to the audience. He grabs the microphone with his right hand and flings the cord out with his left, something he will do almost continually during the show. He will also move about constantly, which makes him appear nervous and a little ill at ease. He is a wispy, sparrowlike figure on stage; his long red curly hair trails over his collar, black-rimmed glasses circle large eyes and set off a slightly confused face. He looks lost.

"I think I will review for you some of the outstanding features of my private life and put them in perspective. Then we'll have a brief question-and-answer period and evaluate them," he tells the audience.

The material is not new. Most of it was written between 1962 and 1968, and to prepare for these shows Woody has

5

listened over and over to his three record albums to get the words and timing right. The audience doesn't mind. Most of them, in fact, have never heard any of his material before and were not familiar with him until about 1968, when he started making films. Everyone is laughing right away, which is what they've come to do.

Woody talks about growing up in Brooklyn; about organizing the workers in his father's store, going on strike, and driving him out of business; about a cousin who sells mutual funds and whose wife has orgasmic insurance ("If her husband fails to satisfy her sexually, Mutual of Omaha has to pay her every month."); about his sexual prowess ("On my wedding night my wife stopped in the middle of everything and gave me a standing ovation."); about his ex-wife ("She was coming home late at night and she was violated. That's how they put it in the New York papers; she was violated. And they asked me to comment on it. I said, 'Knowing my ex-wife, it probably was not a moving violation.' ").

The jokes are what he calls "verbal cartoons." They have a surreal, fantastic quality to them, but even so they are somehow believeable, when Woody describes them, as events that could happen, if only to him. While most of the material is a kind of long narrative, there are throwaways interspersed, such as one about a girl he met in Europe who ran away to Venice, became a streetwalker, and drowned.

A little more than halfway through the act he stops for a moment and pulls out a pocket watch. "Pardon me a moment while I check the time," he says. "They're very punctilious about time here and I can hear the band padding in behind me." He looks at the watch and holds it up,

6

as if all 1,200 people could see it. "I don't know if you can see this, but it's a very handsome watch." He brings his hand down and looks closely at the watch. "Has marble inlay. It makes me look Italian. My grandfather, on his deathbed, sold me this watch." If the audience believed for a moment that he really did have to check the time, they know now they've been had. What they don't know is that the line gives him a chance to see how he really is doing against time. He is supposed to do forty-five minutes; that joke should come at about twenty-eight minutes into the act. If it comes before that, he'll have to stretch the rest of the material as much as he can while protecting the laughs. Unlike most comedians, he cannot just go on and on; he feels obliged to do material he has worked out and which he knows is good.

He puts the watch away and soon is telling the audience: "I was kidnapped once. I was standing in front of my school yard and a black sedan pulls up and two guys get out and they say to me, do I want to go away with them to a land where everybody is fairies and elves and I can have all the comic books I want, and chocolate buttons, and wax lips, you know. And I said, yes. And I got into the car with them, 'cause I figured, what the hell, I was home anyhow that weekend from college. And they drive me off and they send a ransom note to my parents. And my father has bad reading habits. So he got into bed that night with the ransom note and he read half of it and he got drowsy and he fell asleep. Meanwhile they take me to New Jersey bound and gagged. And my parents finally realize that I'm kidnapped and they snap into action immediately: They rent out my room. The ransom note says for my father to leave a thousand dollars in a hollow tree

7

in New Jersey. He has no trouble raising the thousand dollars, but he gets a hernia carrying the hollow tree. The F.B.I. surround the house. 'Throw the kid out,' they say, 'give us your guns and come out with your hands up.' The kidnappers say, 'We'll throw the kid out, but let us keep our guns and get to our car.' The F.B.I. says, 'Throw the kid out, we'll let you get to your car but give us your guns.' The kidnappers say, 'We'll throw the kid out, but let us keep our guns, we don't have to get to our car.' The F.B.I. says, 'Keep the kid. . . .' Wait a minute, I've screwed this up. The F.B.I. decides to lob in tear gas. But they don't have tear gas. So several of the agents put on the death scene from *Camille*. Tear-stricken, my abductors give themselves up. They're sentenced to fifteen years on a chain gang and they escape, twelve of them chained together at the ankle, getting by the guards posing as an immense charm bracelet.

"Here's a story you're not going to believe," he tells them. "I shot a moose once. I was hunting in upstate New York and I shot a moose. And I strap him onto the fender of my car, and I'm driving home along the West Side Highway. But what I didn't realize was that the bullet did not penetrate the moose. It just creased his scalp, knocking him unconscious. And I'm driving through the Holland Tunnel and the moose woke up. So I'm driving with a live moose on my fender and the moose is signaling for a turn. And there's a law in New York State against driving with a conscious moose on your fender, Tuesdays, Thursdays, and Saturdays. And I'm very panicky. And then it hits me—some friends of mine are having a costume party. I'll go. I'll take the moose. I'll ditch him at the party. It won't be my responsibility. So I drive up to the party and I knock on the door. The moose is next to me. My host comes to the door. I say, 'Hello, you know the Solomons.' We enter. The moose mingles. Did very well. Scored. Some guy was trying to sell him insurance for an hour and a half. Twelve o'clock comes, they give out the prizes for the best costume of the night. First prize goes to the Berkowitzes, a married couple dressed as a moose. The moose comes in second. The moose is furious. He and the Berkowitzes lock antlers in the living room. They knock each other unconscious. Now, I figure, here's my chance. I grab the moose, strap him on my fender, and shoot back to the woods. But I've got the Berkowitzes. So I'm driving along with two Jewish people on my fender. And there's a law in New York State, Tuesdays, Thursdays, and especially Saturday. . . . The following morning, the Berkowitzes wake up in the woods in a moose suit. Mr. Berkowitz is shot, stuffed, and mounted at the New York Athletic Club. And the joke is on them, 'cause it's restricted."

The audience is convulsed with laughter for the last three-quarters of the story, and Woody is about to quit. But first he tells them that "I came home one night some months ago and I went to the closet in my bedroom and a moth ate my sport jacket. He was laying there on the floor, nauseous. It's a yellow and green sport jacket. Little fat moth lying there groaning, part of the sleeve hanging out of his mouth. I gave him two plain brown socks. I said, 'Eat one now, eat one in half an hour.' "

Finally he tells them that he's going to go and get dinner. He pulls his room key from his pocket and looks at it a second. "I was walking around the casino yesterday and I saw a really beautiful girl. I dropped my room key in her pocketbook. Twenty minutes later I went up to my room . . . and my typewriter was gone. Goodnight."

Onstage he has appeared just as the audience has come to expect: nervous, a little forgetful, a small man beset by huge obstacles. Nothing could be further from the truth. He is nervous onstage only until the first couple of laughs —a few seconds. The pacing about, the flicking of the microphone cord, the seeming momentary forgetting of a line, the apparently spontaneous taking off of his glasses and rubbing his eyes while delivering a punchline are all part of the act. He knows where he is at every moment and exactly what he's doing. Every good comic does. They have done their routines hundreds of times, polishing them until they sound new with every performance. Woody says that that kind of knowledge of the material can have its drawbacks.

"Sometimes I catch myself just going by rote, looking down at a girl in the audience, thinking about the show I'm going to after I'm done. When I first started, if I did a show for three hundred people and another show three hours later where one of them might be there, I was ashamed to use the same material. But I've found people like the old material. It takes about a year to write a new act, so I don't mind doing this now. I never improvised onstage until the last year and a half of performing, and then I started asking for questions from the audience because I found, simply, that my standards for material are very high, and it's very hard for me to get a lot of time, so I really condense it. I'll write hours of material and wind up with thirty-five minutes that are really funny, where the jokes keep ripping off each other. I found I was always short-timed and I started asking for questions from

10

the audience. As it turned out, the questions were the best part of my act because the material couldn't stand up against reality. So now I think I could go out there and very nicely do a show that is almost all questions with occasional material because of the situation. They accept me. Acceptance is more important for a comedian than for other performers. They laugh at me all the time. I don't have to prove anything. They think things are funny even if they're not that funny. [An audience that has accepted a comedian will also laugh at jokes they don't understand. Bob Hope was performing one time in England and the punchline to a joke was the word "motel." When Hope said "motel" everyone laughed. But one of his writers asked the woman next to him if anyone knew what a motel was. "No," she said. "Then why are they laughing?" he asked. "Because they know it's the end of the joke and they know he's funny," she answered.]

"One of the most popular routines I did was getting robbed and mugged in my lobby. There are routines and there's talk. I prefer talk. The kidnapping thing is a routine. Of all the routines the moose thing is probably most popular. It was a happy accident. It's not long, only about two and a half minutes, so it's hard to get bored in it. It has a beginning, a middle, and an end. It goes uphill; I was able to wring twist after twist after twist out of it till the end, so it keeps going and doesn't die. It doesn't depend on jokes. It gets the audience involved in this premise, this concept, and they go with it."

How does Woody condense his material and decide what to keep in the act? "One of the most successful things I ever did was the stuff about the damaged pet shop and the ant. ["I couldn't get a dog because it was too

11

much. And they finally opened up in my neighborhood in Flatbush a damaged pet shop. They had damaged pets at discount. You could get a bent pussycat if you wanted . . . a straight camel. I got a dog that stuttered. The cats would give him a tough time and he would go b-b-b-b-b-b-b-bow wow."] I still get that from the audience more than anything else. People say, 'Do you have a dog?' Those terrible kinds of lead-ins that they give you that I invariably cringe from. I was home in my apartment and I was walking around working out these jokes—I was going to use them that night at the Village Gate—and I always wanted a dog and my parents got me an ant, and I called it Spot, and I thought, God, that's so funny to me. And I did it that night at the Village Gate and it got nothing. I did it the next night and it got nothing and I dropped it completely out of my act. Then about ten months later I came across it in my notes and I said, Jesus, that is so funny, and I started doing it and it started to jell. It became one of the biggest laughs and things I ever did. I have no idea why those things ever happen. I can only surmise that you have to give the material a fair shake at the time and you have to deliver it with confidence.

"The place to test new material is the prime show on Saturday night. Other comics would always say, well, on the late shows Tuesday and Wednesday I put my new stuff in. And I figured, Jesus, it's hard enough to go over with your *best* stuff on a rainy Tuesday. So I'd always try to break in new material in Vegas or someplace like that. The hardest thing is to do it with confidence, to do the new stuff like it's your old stuff. I get out there and bludgeon them to death with my old stuff. I just know how to say it. But if you're tentative with the new stuff you screw

12

yourself out of laughs left and right. It's like offering up a loser. You've got to offer it up as though it's a winner."

Just what it is that makes a man get up on a stage and tell stories to people in order to get them to laugh is hard to say. Vanity has something to do with it for certain; a need to communicate and be accepted is something else. Comics talk a lot about "killing" their audiences or wanting them to "die laughing," so probably there is some hostility, too. "I found people looked better when they laughed," Mort Sahl once said, so beautification of the species may be another factor.

It is a bizarre talent at best. There are few who can do it well—far fewer than can do brain surgery, for instance.

Whatever it is that makes someone a stand-up comedian, there are only a small number of them who are truly original and who set tones and standards of comedy that other good comics take off from and bad comics try, with small success, to imitate. Mort Sahl is one of the originals and one of the major influences on Woody. To examine his brand of humor is to learn a good bit about Woody's.

When Woody first saw Sahl in 1954, "I was a TV writer with hopes of writing for Broadway. Sahl was an inspiring comedian. My interest in nightclub performing was nil until I saw him. Then it occurred to me that, 'Hey, you could be a comedian because you have the equipment; that is a very valid way to express yourself.' I realized performing wouldn't mean abandoning plays forever."

Jonathan Miller once said Sahl's act is about "the dilemma of metropolitan man drowning in the surroundings he himself fashioned." It is also the act of a comic

13

original who happened to change the way stand-up comedy was presented.

In 1953, when Sahl began, comedians were visual burlesque-style clowns who wore tuxedos, talked about their mothers-in-law, and came on at places like the Copacabana surrounded by chorus girls in big dance numbers. Sahl was and is strictly a verbal comedian relying more on subtlety and wit than physical funniness combined with verbal gags.

Woody thought Sahl "was the best thing I ever saw. He was like Charlie Parker in jazz. There was a need for a revolution, everybody was ready for the revolution, but some guy had to come along who could perform the revolution and be great. Mort was the one. He was like the tip of the iceberg. Underneath were all the other people who came along: Lenny Bruce, Nichols and May, all the Second City players. I'm not saying that these people wouldn't have happened anyway, but Mort was the vanguard of the group that had an enormous renaissance of nightclub comedy that ended not long after Bill Cosby and I came along. He totally restructured comedy. His jokes are laid down with such guile. He changed the rhythm of jokes. He had different content, surely, but the revolution was in the way he laid the jokes down."

Sahl, of course, did not set out to start a revolution. "It wasn't exactly nobility that got me going," he says. "I was twenty-six. I was working on a novel and introducing things for a theater group. I was out of the service, I was out of work, and I was out of gas. I was really angry that anybody told me [that my kind of humor] couldn't be done. It became an end in itself. There's no problem that

14

there will be a guy that comes along. The problem is in building a constituency.

"My girl friend was in Berkeley, I was starving there, and she said, 'Why don't you try out at the "hungry i"?' Then she said something very wise: 'If they understand you, you're home free; and if they don't, they'll pretend that it's whimsical humor.' Which is really a veiled attack on phony intellectuals that was quite prophetic. So what I did was ask for an audition, and they gave me one of one night. And I packed the house with students. I loaded it. Shades of Ron Ziegler. And I had them laugh. And like any tutored group, it lacked spontaneity. I got up and said hello and they laughed. [Enrico Banducci, who ran the "hungry i," was apparently not taken in by Sahl's audience-packing. He hired him, really, on the basis of two jokes: "Senator McCarthy does not question what you say so much as your right to say it;" and a comparison between the Eisenhower jacket; which had a lot of "multidirectional zippers," and the McCarthy jacket. "The McCarthy jacket is just like the Eisenhower jacket, except it has an extra zipper to go across the mouth."]

"Banducci hired me for seventy-five dollars to fill in for a singer named Dorothy Baker for a week. I thought I was really home free. Then I got up on stage on Monday night without my audience. Dead. People started throwing pennies on stage, peanuts. I was shaken. That's how the newspaper was born in my act. I wrote my key lines on paper and stapled them in the newspaper, because the silence would make me forget my lines. Then I'd say, 'I see in the paper . . .' but under the harsh lights I couldn't read my own writing. And every once in a while I would digress because I had no discipline. And when I digressed, I got my first laugh."

There were other refinements in the act. "I took off my coat at Banducci's urging. I took off my tie. And then it occurred to me, you musn't look like any member of the society you're criticizing. What could I be? I was twenty-six. I went out and got myself a pair of blue denims and a blue sweater and a white button-down shirt open at the neck: graduate student. Which I was. And I went out there and did it and it worked. It let the audience relax. It had never been done. I used to get arguments from [traditionalists] about the sweater. Here I was attacking the President and I was getting arguments about the sweater. These great rules I've violated. Now, of course, it's reversed itself. Nobody talks to me like I'm a comedian. It's like I'm a senator. I've had people yell at me that I'm a liar, I'm crazy or subversive, but I've never had a guy walk up and say rationally to me, 'It's true that espionage is an issue, that war is an issue, but who in the hell are you to adjudicate it?' In 1964 I was working at the Sands Hotel in Las Vegas and a lot of comedians would gather in the lounge when their shows were over: Jackie Leonard, Shelly Berman, Don Rickles. They asked some questions about the election coming up like I was a profes-sor. Then Jackie Leonard asked if the conventioneers in town were as bad an audience for the other comedians as for him. And as they talked of comedy all I saw were a bunch of backs. They had all turned away from me, as though it was none of my concern. I was a United States Senator visiting Nevada."

There is little difference between Sahl onstage and off; he constantly exudes his personality, sensitivity, and out-

16

rage, and many people in show business think of him as an intellectual. (Bob Hope once introduced him at the Academy Awards: "Here he is, the favorite of nuclear physicists everywhere.") They are wrong. Sahl is an intelligent man and, certainly, as Robert Rice wrote in *The New Yorker*, "the first entertainer in years who contrived to smuggle his brains past a velvet rope." But he is not an intellectual. With his farraginous material he is like a graduate student who hasn't focused on his major, an incipient failure as a Ph.D. who is no threat to anyone. He doesn't talk about Möbius strips or quantum physics or Chaucer. Rather he speaks with intelligence on common events.

"I submit to you I've been called an intellectual more times than you can count," he says. "I was a sort of 'C' student in college. To me an intellectual is someone like Bertrand Russell or Oppenheimer or Einstein. I'm not an intellectual. It shines great on show business that I would be called an intellectual. After all, I *quote* intellectuals. Fifty years ago, I would have been a reporter with some promise on a newspaper, maybe." ("Nonintellectual comedians try desperately to be intellectual," Woody says. "Intellectual comedians try desperately not to be. Sahl wants nothing more than to have massive communication.")

Woody, too, has been called an intellectual comedian, which is as wrong a label for him as it is for Sahl—though, like Sahl, he is an intelligent man.

"People have always thought of me as an intellectual comedian, and I'm not. I'm a one-liner comic like Bob Hope and Henny Youngman. I do the wife jokes. I make faces. I'm a comedian in the classic style."

What makes Woody different and original is his personality and outlook. Like Sahl he makes intellectual references and esoteric comments in his act ("I took all the abstract philosophy courses in college, like Truth and Beauty and Advanced Truth and Beauty, and Intermediate Truth, Introduction to God, Death 101. I was thrown out of N.Y.U. my freshman year. I cheated on my Metaphysics final. I looked within the soul of the boy sitting next to me.") but he is really in many ways a traditional comic—a fact that is often overlooked because the standard subjects—wife, family, pets, and so on—are presented in a very idiosyncratic, original, surreal context.

"People reacted to Sahl just as they did to every great turn of art," Woody says. "He had all the symptoms of every modern development of art. He was suddenly this great genius that appeared. He himself was a great funny man. They didn't know that the art was inborn in him, in his intonation. People would say, 'I don't like him, he doesn't do anything, he's not funny. I do that all the time and nobody pays me—I sit at home and talk. And he's not doing any comedy.' It was just the kind of thing where you could see art critics saying years ago, 'What is this terrible impressionist painting?' He had all the great qualities. It doesn't surprise me that his records sound good now, because he's fun to hear because of all that energy."

Sahl's free-flowing energy on the stage, and the fact that a good portion of his act is improvised and changed all the time, is in almost direct contrast to Woody's performing. Seemingly spontaneous mannerisms are generally a part of Woody's act—he will take off his glasses and rub his eyes at the same lines practically every time, and he will appear to have gotten confused over what comes next in the same story at the same point in each performance, all to good effect and the enhancement of his material. Woody is much more controlled with his material, as he is in his life, and with his own reasons. Where Sahl is primarily a talker who seldom writes out his material, Woody is primarily a writer who has the discipline to write and rewrite until the joke is as near to perfect as he can make it. They have two wholly different styles and senses of values that match their personalities.

"I put no premium on improvising," Woody says. "It's nice if you feel in the mood but it's not a big deal. But I do improvise when I write the act. I don't want to improvise in front of an audience because I feel they should have the benefit of perfected material."

After two weeks and twenty-eight shows in Las Vegas, Woody leaves with relief, flying to San Francisco where he opens that night for six shows in four days at a theater-in-the-round twenty miles down the peninsula. He is tired and fed up with performing. He seems to have forgotten how tedious and boring it can be on the road. He checks into his suite at the Fairmont Hotel and goes downstairs to a press conference one of his two managers, Charles Joffe, has arranged. He is wearing what he wore onstage in Las Vegas, what he wore onstage in Chicago, what he will wear onstage here: the same saddle shoes and corduroy trousers and sport coat he wears every day, on and off stage. The only addition is a khaki rain hat. He calls it "my disguise hat. It cuts fifty percent of recognition—and my act cuts the other fifty percent."

There is a large turnout. Besides just being a popular entertainer, Woody is well known to the San Francisco media because *Take the Money and Run* and *Play It Again, Sam* were filmed there and he played the "hungry i" a lot in the early '60s when he was just beginning as a stand-up comic. There is a bar and lots of hors d'oeuvres. The reporters drink quickly and jostle for the jumbo shrimp before Woody comes.

Woody walks in and sits down behind a table with some microphones on it. He is a little put off by the idea of a conference; it was arranged so he would not have to give numerous individual interviews, which he would like even less.

"When I think of all the trivia that's going to be discussed here!" he says.

"You're the first honest newsmaker to come through," one of the reporters tells him.

"Have there been a lot of people running for office?" Woody asks. Everyone laughs. "I'm just a show business personality who's going to the, uh. . . ."

"Circle Star Theatre," someone calls out.

"To the Circle Star Theatre and make a few jokes."

Only a few of the thirty-three people at the conference ask questions. They are about Oriental films ("They're hard to sit through, but I liked *Throne of Blood.*"); violence in films ("I love violence if it's well done. I think *Bonnie and Clyde* is a masterpiece."); and his fans ("I never experience a sense of confidence about my fans. I don't know who they are or where they are. Many cities wouldn't even book *Take the Money and Run.* There were only two theaters, so they showed the Paul Newman and Dustin Hoffman pictures.").

The conference breaks up. On the way out a representative of Warner Books gives out paperback copies of

20

Getting Even, a collection of Woody's humorous prose, most of which appeared in *The New Yorker.* Woody goes upstairs to get a shower and rest before dinner and the half-hour drive to the theater.

The San Francisco shows do not sell as well as everyone hoped, though Woody is not surprised. "I've never sold out in my life. That would surprise me more." The theater holds three thousand; average attendance is just under two thousand. A likely reason is the theater's location: too far away from the city, where Woody's greatest support probably is. On Friday night it rains and the house is only half full.

"Where were they?" asks Woody, who seldom seems concerned about the size of the house, while riding in the car on the way back to town.

A friend tells him that last week at a party at author Alvin Toffler's home, "He was reading *Getting Even* aloud and people were falling on the floor."

"Yeah?" Woody says. "There were probably more people at his house."

Woody is buoyed by going directly to Earthquake McGoon's and playing clarinet for a couple of sets with Turk Murphy's band. There is a good crowd, many of whom have come to hear him play, some of them from the audience at the theater. One of them is a twenty-two-year-old would-be comedy writer who keeps pestering Woody between sets with ideas he has for him. (It has been an odd day for fans. That afternoon a young man dressed in a get-up like the sperm suit Woody wore in *Sex* appeared at his door at the Fairmont and was quickly turned away.) Although he does not smile during the sets, for the first time that day Woody looks as if he is enjoying

21

himself. He is clearly caught up in the music and glad of it.

After the band packs up he goes for a chocolate sundae at Enrico's, the coffee house-restaurant owned by Enrico Banducci, who has given up the "hungry i." Banducci's relationships with performers were normally less than cordial—he does not think much of Woody's talents, for instance—although he hired Mort Sahl for long periods at a time when his popularity lulled. He gave Barbra Streisand her first West Coast job after she yelled at him, "Hire me, you jerk! You never hire no-names." Banducci could have been created by Damon Runyon, so he is hard not to like in spite of what he says or does. He once gave Nichols and May a $5,000 check as a bonus because business had been so good, but the check bounced; after that Jack Rollins, their original manager and Woody's other manager, made sure Woody was paid in cash every night.

Banducci is not at his place, though; nor, in fact, are many people, since it is cold and nearly 2:00 A.M. The waiter takes the order and comes back quickly with a chocolate sundae with no whipped cream. "You still like it without the whipped cream, yes?" he asks Woody. Woody is surprised the waiter remembers after so many years and thanks him. He likes San Francisco better than Las Vegas for every possible reason.

"I was twenty-six when I first played here. I was assured that this place loves comics, that I'd be a hit. I died at the 'hungry i.' Lenny Bruce opened the same night I did. Drew huge crowds. The first time Vaughn Meader came to see me, we stood on the steps together. I wondered what he was going to do after his 'First Family' album, and he told me that he had another coming out. 'If only twenty percent of the people who bought the last one buy it, it will be a million seller,' he said. But I don't think they did.

"Cavett and I were with Mort Sahl the night President Kennedy was shot. Sahl was mimicking an agent who has a brainstorm in a time of crisis, knowing what his client has been doing successfully may now no longer be acceptable because of the crisis, saying, 'Mort, baby, *you* can't do political jokes anymore—but a ventriloquist's dummy could.' There's such deprecating sarcasm in Sahl's voice; he's such a great mimic. He was the first to do jokes where an explanation is required first, like the lead of a Perelman story, because you couldn't laugh at the routine without knowing the facts. Details first, then the routine, like, 'I see Kissinger's gone to Hanoi.' Other people did jokes based on what you already know. And there's such art in his voice, the inflection that he and Groucho have. And Hope. When Hope says it, it comes out funny. When Picasso draws it, it looks beautiful on the page. In the wake of Sahl, every comedian thought he had to be political. In the first piece *The New York Times* did on me, Arthur Gelb said I was the only comic without a Kennedy joke. Then David Brinkley commented on it on NBC."

A pretty girl comes over to the table. "Are you really Woody Allen?" she asks, a little nervously.

Woody nods.

"Well, I'm a Playboy Club Bunny and anytime you want to come to the Club I can get you in for free. Just tell them Julie sent you."

Woody thanks her and she leaves. Such naïveté must be its own reward. Woody shakes his head. "Now that'd be a thrill, getting in free at the Playboy Club."

23

The next day there is another press conference, this time with newspaper editors from the colleges in the area. Inexplicably, college editors in interviewing him have always been the hardest of any media people on Woody, even though what they have written has almost always been favorable, so he is somewhat apprehensive. Eight people show up at his suite. His philosophy about interviews is consistent and unbeatable: "If you don't lie, you don't have to remember what you say."

Within a couple of minutes it is clear that this group of editors, anyway, is anything but hostile. A couple of them gush. Amazingly, not one of them knows who either S.J. Perelman or Robert Benchley is; three say they've heard the name of one or the other. Someone asks how Woody feels about being a comic. "I'm fortunate to have been born in an era when comics are valued. What if I was born an Indian in the old west? How many Navajos do you know who are comics?" The editors leave, along with the ubiquitous representative of Warner Books, and Woody drives back down to the theater for the two shows that night.

The dressing room is like a small living room in a middle-class Ohio suburb: a sofa, a couple of matching chairs, a color TV, and hardware-store sheetwood paneling. There is a mirror off to the side, a bar in the rear of the room, and a small bathroom. On the counter in front of the mirror are gifts and letters from fans: a six-foot loaf of sourdough bread, compliments of the regional sales manager for a bakery; script outlines for wholly unsuitable movies; several invitations to "casual" lunches, dinners, brunches, and cocktail parties with "just a few close friends." Each has almost identical sentiments: "I know you like privacy and we promise not to bother you with a lot of questions. Hotels must be very boring after a while, and we would be more than happy to have you just come and relax. You don't even have to be funny."

The best letter is from a girl who wrote him three years ago after seeing *What's New, Pussycat?* because she didn't understand the line, "Send twelve loaves of bread and one Boy Scout uniform to the Marquis de Sade room." "You told me I should read Krafft-Ebing," the girl writes, "so I read it from cover to cover but found no reference to twelve loaves of bread and a Boy Scout uniform. I thought maybe there was another volume, so I went to the Stanford University Department of Psychology and asked if they had Krafft-Ebing there. 'Does he teach here?' they asked me. What do I do now?"

The late singer Jim Croce begins the shows, so it is nearly nine o'clock when Woody goes on for the first time. The house is pretty good but they aren't a great laughing audience. Woody gets to where he pulls the watch out. He looks at it and groans. He's four minutes faster than he should be. The laughter picks up a bit when he tells them about his grandfather selling him the watch. He tells them about being kidnapped and then asks if there are any questions.

"What is one of your biggest thrills in life?"

"Jumping naked into a vat of cold Roosevelt dimes." (He had a question-and-answer session on one TV special. Billy Graham was a guest, so someone asked Woody what his greatest sin was. "Having impure thoughts about Art Linkletter.")

Between shows Woody turns down the theater mana-ger's offer of a dinner from their restaurant and asks instead if it is possible to get a bucket of Colonel Sanders' fried chicken with a lot of honey on the side. It is. He flicks on the TV and a picture of woods by a lake comes on. In a matter of seconds he says, "*A Place in the Sun,* directed by George Stevens." Montgomery Clift comes into the picture. He's right. He says that Shelley Winters deserves what's about to happen to her and that Elizabeth Taylor isn't as pretty as she was in *National Velvet,* though he can see why most men like her. The chicken comes. Shelley Winters drowns. Clift looks more and more doomed; Dreiser was an uncompromising writer. Taylor is sent to a boarding school, Clift to meet his Maker. Woody does some card tricks to pass the time.

The stage manager knocks on the door and says there are two pretty young women who want to see Woody. Woody shrugs his shoulders; who knows, one of them may be good to take out later. The women come in. They are from the Midwest but are living in San Francisco. They are in their twenties and pretty but excruciatingly dull and without humor. Woody's hopefulness quickly vanishes. They are not particularly enthused either. "We thought you'd be a little wilder," one of them says. They go. Woody does some more card tricks. "Only three more shows. I can barely wait."

The audience for the second show is only about fifteen hundred, but they laugh louder and more quickly than the first. Woody believes two things about audiences: they are always with a performer at the beginning, hoping he does well; and if they don't laugh a lot, it is their fault, not his. But he will go after an unresponsive audience to try to get them to laugh.

When he checks his watch he's running nearly six minutes behind the first show. He comes offstage enthused for the first time in the engagement, though part of it is because he knows that there are only two more shows tomorrow and then he has three days off, the first in over a month. ("To do what? Brood uninterruptedly.")

2.
"I had to struggle to keep alive in that kind of company."

In the spring of 1952, Walter Winchell and Earl Wilson began receiving unsolicited jokes, postmarked Brooklyn and signed "Woody Allen." Sixteen-year-old Alan Stewart Konigsberg had changed his name because "it had all the glamorous appeal of show business one imagines in Flatbush," and it kept people at Midwood High School from saying they had seen his name in the papers, which he didn't want. What he did want was a decision about what to do with his life and he hoped that writing jokes for the columns might help him make that decision. He and his friends were at the point where they had to make college and career choices, and his parents wanted him to be a pharmacist. But that required years of study and Woody hated school so much that he regularly played hooky for a week at a time. He considered becoming a bookmaker, a confidence swindler, a cowboy, a gangster, or perhaps an F.B.I. agent, and he toyed with the idea of being on the periphery of the medical profession by running an optometrist's shop with his friend Mickey Rose; but along with "not holding a whit of interest for me," it also required more schooling. What he really wanted was a job where he could take days off and go to ball games. He began submitting jokes and within three weeks they were being published.

Woody chose writing because it was the one area in school that he liked and in which he did well. In the first grade the teacher was reading his compositions aloud. "By the fifth grade I had some innate knowledge of how to write funny, so much so that I would be doing references to Freud and sex, too, without knowing who he and what it really was but sensing how to use them correctly. Teachers would read my compositions and bring other teachers into the room and they'd read them together and point at me."

By the seventh grade he knew the act of every comedian of stature from listening to them on the radio and seeing them in the movies. He especially liked Bob Hope "because of his greatness as a comic and his snotty one-liners." Other, unknown comics he watched at the Flatbush Theatre, one of the last vaudeville houses. Going every Saturday and sitting through five acts at least once, he copied routines on his candy box and memorized them. Whenever he was called on in class he delivered bits and routines. He would probably have been a great vaudevillian, had it lasted; there is, he thinks, "a little gene in me that craves vaudeville. I like telling jokes and doing the two tap dance steps that I know." When Ed Sullivan's show became the last stand of vaudeville, he would always watch it. Years later, in a corduroy suit and narrow tie, he played the show, and, when Sullivan congratulated him at the end of his act, Woody mimicked Hope's snottiness and told him, "You do a good job."

The days he played hooky had a predictable pattern. He would leave his home at Avenue K and 15th Street after a breakfast of a lot of chocolate cake and milk, or he'd go to the corner drugstore and have "one of those pound cakes cut into thirds without removing the cellophane, the way those guys can do it, and good coffee," and instead of walking to school he would ride the subway forty-five minutes across Brooklyn and over the Manhattan Bridge to Times Square. He spent hours in the Automat drinking coffee or walking around the theater district. He went to magic shops and bought books on card and magic tricks. They became his textbooks, those magic books, and for every hour that he didn't study algebra he spent six learning and practicing dealing from the bottom of the deck. It was the perfect avocation for the shy boy who believed the ad that said, "Learn magic; be popular at parties." Magic, he felt, "fit into everything I needed at the time. It kept me isolated from the world. It was so much better than school, which was boring, frightening. The whole thing was ugly. I never had the answers. I never did the homework."

So he escaped into the sleight of hand of magic and, more important, into the sleight of mind of movies. He spent weekends and many weekdays too in movie theaters, but not as just another stunned, mouth-breathing escapist into fantasy. Without knowing the terms, he had a discriminating sense of good and bad filmmaking. Certainly he watched and loved every cheapie that came along: the Whistler and Charlie Chan movies and the crime and doctor pictures. But when he thought back later to the films that impressed him in his adolescence, it would be films like Ernst Lubitsch's or Preston Sturges's that came to mind.

When he wasn't practicing tricks or watching movies, he was at the radio, listening to Jack Benny, "Duffy's Tavern," "The Great Gildersleeve," and "Fibber McGee and Molly"—every comedy show; as with the vaudevillians, he could quote them all.

Woody Allen was born on December 1, 1935, the first child of Martin Konigsberg of Brooklyn and Nettie Cherrie of Manhattan's Lower East Side, who were married and living in Flatbush, a community he would later describe as "the heart of the Old World: their values in life are God and carpeting." Until he was fifteen, Woody never knew exactly what his father did for a living—only that there were little businesses here and there which involved, among other things, being a cab driver, a jewelry engraver, and a waiter in Sammy's Bowery Follies. His mother was a bookkeeper in a Manhattan florist shop. He liked ball games and pinochle and western movies; she, romantic movies, shopping, and talking with her sisters.

When Woody was eight, Martin and Nettie had a daughter whose hair is slightly redder than Woody's, whose face is slightly rounder, who is altogether pretty. "Letty and I are just one of those things that are luck," Woody says. "I liked her as soon as I met her." Letty in turn adored Woody. She became his companion, his audience for magic tricks, his fan. ("She was precocious.") The

31

age difference between them precluded any squabbling, even when they shared a bedroom for a few years until Woody left home when she was ten. Now Letty has a son who also adores Woody but has small regard for his fame. He sees his uncle on the screen and assumes everyone else's is too.

Fame in Old World Brooklyn is not to be found in show business. Regardless of the success, there is always another contract to get, another deal to be made, another show to, God willing, do. Not that being President of the United States would be any better: four, maybe eight years, and then what? Security is Brooklyn's idea of fame, and doctors are secure and teachers are secure and rabbis are secure. But comedians and Presidents are not, and if today Woody gave up the career that has made him known around the world, that has brought him a duplex penthouse on Fifth Avenue and a limousine that takes him to wherever he doesn't want to walk; if he gave up the career that has made him rich enough never to have to work again and enrolled in a teacher's program at New York University, his parents would probably be relieved because his future would at last be assured.

Nothing about his home life suggested his unnatural interest in and talent for comedy, and nothing about it instilled the unusual interest in art and music that sent him to Manhattan. (The people in his community went to Manhattan only to see their doctors.) He had, in fact, a rather ordinary Brooklyn boyhood. He liked fishing and he was good at sports—he played second base on a Police Athletic League team and he entered Golden Gloves competition, but withdrew when his parents disapproved. His major quirk was that he was a fan not of the

32

Brooklyn Dodgers but rather of the New York Giants "from the time I was old enough to root. They were a big home-run team, and I just liked them." He especially liked Willie Mays. To him Mays is "the closest thing to a miracle or a magician. We hope that there is some kind of magic and we're all taking a piece of him. It's the confluence of all the good things that a guy like that can come out of the universe." He remembers standing in front of his TV set in 1951 when Mays got his first hit, a home run. Woody is a tremendous sports fan, especially of the New York Knicks. (The only reason he has ever wrapped a day's shooting on a picture early was to be home in time for an important game.) He has other heroes, most of them black: Sugar Ray Robinson, Louis Armstrong, and Earl "The Pearl" Monroe, whom he calls "poetic." Although "if I could pick up a stone and become Walt Frazier, I wouldn't hesitate a second," he would not like to be George S. Kaufman or one of the Marx Brothers, his other heroes. But Willie Mays and Mays alone did to him what Ingmar Bergman does to him as a filmmaker and Marlon Brando does to him as an actor—made him feel that there was magic other than what he studied in his books.

In his last term at Midwood, David O. Alber Associates, a public relations firm that handled celebrities including Bob Hope, Arthur Murray, Guy Lombardo, and Sammy Kaye, hired him to write clever lines that could be attributed to their clients and sent to the columns. An assistant of Earl Wilson's, Marty Burden, had recommended Woody, who was hired at twenty-five dollars per week for twenty hours of work. His jokes—he turned in fifty a day —soon were ideal and his name began appearing in the columns nearly every day. Wilson even asked if he could use some of the jokes himself and Woody felt he was in "the heart of show business." When he began college at New York University, his salary was raised to forty dollars per week.

He registered for motion picture production at NYU because he thought it was "a dumb, cinch course." He attended the films regularly but the classes only once in a while, and he failed motion picture production. He also failed Beginning Spanish (he had had two years in high school) and English (he wrote funny essays and there was no room for nonsense); at the end of the first semester, he had failed out of the college of his choice. He enrolled in night school courses at City College, "in an effort to keep my mother from opening her wrists," but he had no more success with motion picture production there. He gave up what he had never seriously undertaken and started writing jokes full time.

His picture once appeared in the papers as well as his jokes. Alber called on him when he needed someone to be shown with Guy Lombardo when *Cosmopolitan* did a story on his "surprising" appeal to young people. Woody and his first real girl friend, fifteen-year-old Harlene Rosen, were sent to the Roosevelt Grill to be photographed.

After about a year, Alber started having trouble—celebrities, among them Hope and Sammy Kaye, left the agency. Without celebrities there wasn't much use for writers, and so they were the next to go. Gene Shefrin, Woody's boss, called Woody into his office and did what he had to do as quickly as he could. He fired his best writer with two weeks' severance pay—eighty dollars—and when he finished his ex-best writer told him what he had not had a chance to do until then—that he had been going to quit that day anyway because NBC had made him an offer of $175 a week to join their Writers' Development Program.

Woody had gotten the NBC job through Harvey Meltzer, an agent with William Morris who had wanted to leave and manage writers on his own. Meltzer felt he had proven his legitimacy by landing Woody the NBC job and wanted to become his manager formally. Woody thought Meltzer had done him a favor and agreed to sign a five-year contract, giving Meltzer a twenty-five percent commission. It was the only legal agreement Woody has ever made between himself and a manager. Since 1958, when the contract with Meltzer expired, Jack Rollins and Charles Joffe have made for Woody millions of dollars' worth of deals for a flat fifteen percent on only a hand-shake.

Eighteen-year-old Woody went to Hollywood as the youngest member of the newly formed NBC Writers' Program to save the Colgate Comedy Hour, whose popularity had fallen disastrously ("Deservedly so," says Woody.). The show proved to be beyond redemption, but Woody made a good friend in and was helped professionally by Danny Simon, Neil Simon's brother and the head writer on the Colgate show. Simon took an immediate liking to Woody and his work and told him he "was going to make a lot of money in this business." He was looking for a new partner, he said, and Woody reminded him of Neil, with whom he had written for years; they both wrote great jokes.

After a few months in Hollywood, Woody decided he

wanted to be married. Harlene came out and they were married at the Hollywood Hawaiian Hotel. He was nineteen; she, sixteen. He later referred in his act to his marriage as "The Oxbow Incident" and to their break-up in 1960 as him saying, "Quasimodo, I want a divorce."

"Harlene was kind of tall and nice-figured with dark hair," Woody says. "She's hard to describe physically. Just a nice girl. Tallish. Dark. Medium build. I probably wouldn't recognize her if I saw her now. I haven't seen hide nor hair of her in fifteen years. I'm glad we were married, even though I wasn't too happy while we were and it wasn't all that I thought it would be. Our interests were going in different directions. If we had been born twenty years later, we would simply have moved in together and had a childhood relationship rather than a childhood marriage. It got me out of Brooklyn, though, and out of my parents' house and projected me into reality. Someday I would have had to go through the same thing in one form or another and Harlene was fine. I had a very secure feeling when I was married to her. I did like her, and she did have faith in me. It wouldn't surprise me if she liked my work to this day."

Harlene was the first terminus of Woody's gravitation from Brooklyn to Manhattan. "In my environment where I grew up I was at an early age attracted to a certain type of woman, physically. It's very hard to crystallize exactly the look that turned me on so much, but generally it was almost what you'd call a Jules Feiffer type of girl, the kind that appear in his cartoons with long hair, kind of black-clothed, leather purse-carrying, silver earrings—almost a parody of women today. But at the time I thought they were all beautiful. And I found out so frequently when I

36

used to chase after those girls that they were almost invariably wanting to leave Brooklyn and move to the Village and study art, study music, get into literature, edit films . . . or blow up an office building. When I found that I took out a girl and kind of liked her but she wasn't interested in me because I was a low-life culturally and intellectually, I had to stop reading comic books and start trying to make some effort to explore interests that they had in an effort to survive; all I knew about was baseball. And I found I liked what I saw. I did respond to literature. It wasn't a chore for me after a while. At first I started to read a lot of poetry and literature to educate myself, to boost myself up so I could hold my own. Then I found I liked it. The things the women did led them inevitably to Nietzsche and Trotsky and Beethoven, and I had to struggle to stay alive in that kind of company."

Woody's pursuit of culture was typical of the way he treats new interests. Initial enthusiasm is followed by learning all he can about the subject—whether it is the clarinet or card tricks or billiards or poker—pursuing it until it stops being fun. But only philosophy, magic, and the clarinet have become constant avocations.

Woody's interest in philosophy was coincidental to Harlene's studying it at Hunter College after they moved back to New York from Los Angeles a few months after they were married. Woody spent his time primarily writing occasional material for several well-known performers—Kay Ballard, Carol Channing, Stubby Kaye—and "a million no-name comics" who needed ten funny minutes for Ed Sullivan or "The Tonight Show." But feeling a lack not of school but of schooling, Woody arranged for a tutor to come from Columbia University to help him with a sort of at-home version of a great books course. Beginning with the pre-Socratics, then moving through Plato, Aristotle, Dante, Thomas More, and up to James Joyce, Woody, and often Harlene, read a book a week and discussed it with the tutor.

"I am a voracious reader now," Woody says. "You have to read to stay alive. I read existential philosophy because it mirrors my own anxiety. It's tough, but it has a disciplinary effect and I am trying to grow slowly. Out of this comes vocabulary also. I never had a teacher who made the least impression on me."

While making a good living writing for comics, Woody was becoming more and more dissatisfied with what they were doing with his material. After seeing Mort Sahl perform he realized he could too. One day he mentioned it to Jack Rollins, who never let him forget it.

Rollins is an unforgettable-looking man, thin, with a kind smile, and bags like swamps under his eyes. He looks as though he belongs at a racetrack or high-stakes poker table, where, in fact, he spends much of his time. Unlike most managers, he has a deep affection for and abiding interest in his clients, and he is absolutely honest with them. He is enormously good at discovering and developing raw, new performers—he managed Harry Belafonte, Mike Nichols, and Elaine May when they were just starting. In 1953 he formed a fifty-one/forty-nine-percent partnership with Charles H. Joffe, an ex-agent admittedly "terrible" at booking people, but with a yen to produce films and a talent for helping manage Rollins' growing stable. During the years that Woody was working as a stand-up, Joffe traveled constantly with him, acting as a buffer between Woody and other people, and even went to his show on his own wedding night.

Rollins and Joffe balance each other nicely. "Jack has a tremendous feel for handling artists," Woody says. "One of the big factors in his decisions is, 'Well, if you feel that way, that's very important, even though I think it might be better to do this.' He knows enough to give artists some kind of irrational leeway. Charlie is crackerjack business and has made some fantastic deals for me because he's feisty."

Whenever Rollins and Joffe had listened to Woody reading aloud the material he wrote for other comics, they had always laughed—even though it was being read and not performed. Woody simply came across funny, which is the most vital ingredient for a good comic. Once Woody had expressed an interest in performing, they kept pressing him.

So, on an afternoon in October 1960, Woody told Larry Gelbart, with whom he was writing a TV special, that he was going to perform at the Blue Angel that night in a special audition after Shelly Berman's last set. Berman introduced Woody kindly, saying he was a young television writer who wanted to perform his own material and that he was funny. Woody came out and did thirty minutes of conceptually funny material that the audience loved, but his lack of experience at playing off audiences let them get away. To Gelbart, Woody sounded a little "like Elaine May in drag."

While Rollins knew that Woody was funny, he also knew that the talent to "transfer that to the floor is a universe." It would take two years of performing almost daily in front of often non-laughing, non-comprehending audiences before Woody opened up. Rollins kept him in little clubs where exposure was calculated to have the least shock to a performer, places like the Duplex and the Bon Soir with space for audiences of fifty or sixty.

What Woody had to work on most was how to abandon the notion that if a joke was funny, it would get laughs, no matter that it was being said as though it were being read. "I thought if S.J. Perelman went out and read, say, 'No Starch in the Dhoti, S'il Vous Plaît,' they're going to howl. But that's not what it is at all; it's that the jokes become a vehicle for the person to display a personality or an attitude, just like Bob Hope. You're laughing not at the jokes but at a guy who's looking at Arnold Palmer and saying, 'He's one of my best pupils.' You're laughing at character all the time. I had it backwards. I was totally oriented as a writer."

The two years it took for Woody to develop his character required enormous dedication and determination on his part and an equal amount of faith and encouragement from Rollins and Joffe. To perform full time, Woody abandoned writing for television. His salary dropped from $1,700 a week to $75 a week. Every night Rollins or Joffe or both would go to the Stage Delicatessen or P.J. Clarke's after the show and talk with Woody until early morning about what he was doing well and what needed work. "It's not pleasant to subject myself to this without the reward of response," he told them almost nightly, and often he threatened to quit and go back to writing. But by his own estimation Woody is "a very good practicer; I can practice the clarinet two hours a day in the face of temptation,"

40

and once he decides to do something, he will practice it until he has it.

If his nights were nightmares, getting only occasional laughs, his days were worse, knowing that all that was ahead of him were two or three shows before a generally unenthusiastic audience. He passed the days walking around the city, going to museums, writing a little. When he was working at the Bitter End, he and the club's owner and the cashier spent afternoons telling one another things to say to their psychiatrists, all of whom had offices on the same block. If Woody ever lived on faith and nerve, it was during those two years, until finally, as if by spontaneous combustion, his career ignited.

At about the time he began performing he also began psychoanalysis. When he had tried to re-enter New York University through summer school in 1954, a dean there had suggested he consult a psychiatrist. Woody had protested that he worked steadily writing for television and got on well with people. "Yes, but those theatrical people are all strange," the dean said. In 1959 he began, and he is on his third doctor. His view of the process is wryly pessimistic.

"It's worth it if you can see an end to it. But with me it's like Cole Porter's leg—that endless series of doctors. It's like someone saying to you, 'Well, we're going to try to work together and you must have faith, but we can't guarantee anything and there may be a lot of operations.' Porter went to doctors for twenty-five years and they worked on his leg and finally amputated it. I feel the same thing."

Woody made two friends during his first year of performing who helped him through the tedious, discouraging process. The first was Louise Lasser, a Brandeis University dropout who had been raised in New York and had come back to be a singer. She would eventually become, in more or less this order, one of Woody's best friends, an actress, Woody's wife, his ex-wife, and one of his best friends. The second was a recent Yale graduate, ex-*Time* copy boy and, when he and Woody met, a newly hired joke writer for Jack Paar. His name was Dick Cavett.

Woody and Louise's five-year courtship took place in every cranny of Central Park, in all the museums, in most of the movie houses, and in many of the restaurants in Manhattan.

According to Cavett, "Woody and Louise have always gotten along well; solemnizing it didn't seem to make much difference." After they were married they moved into a huge brownstone like, in Louise's words, "two kids in a castle. We left all the decisions about the house to the housekeeper." One room had a billiard table in it, another was wood paneled and, as Cavett describes it, "looked like the Atheneum Club" except that it was never furnished. At one point it held a jukebox and an electric organ and a pile of cartons. "You had a sense of, 'Oh, you haven't moved in yet.' It was one of the handsomest closets I've seen. The rest of the house was nicely decorated."

Cavett met Woody when he was sent by Paar "to check out this comedian I'd heard about who was writing for Sid Caesar when he was six and had decided to do an act." Woody's effect on Cavett was like Sahl's effect on Woody: "I remember when I heard about Woody I just loved the idea of what he was doing, because it seemed suddenly to ring a bell, like maybe if this works then that's what I'll

42

do. When I called Woody to tell him I was coming, Harlene [this was just before they split up] said he was out for a walk. I even liked the sound of that. I said, 'Yeah, that's what you'd do if you were converting from a writer to a performer.' "

According to Woody, when Cavett went to see him "it was during the period when you would hear people filing out and saying, 'Gee, the guitar player was great, but that comedian.' " But Cavett wasn't one of them. "The minute I walked in that night the sound of the material was so high; I couldn't believe that he could go on so well for twenty minutes with this level of wonderful stuff."

After Woody's set the two of them sat and talked about George S. Kaufman, who had died that day, and then went back to Woody's apartment to talk more. Cavett was taken with the posters on Woody's walls: "From A to Z," a review with Hermione Gingold he had worked on; one for the Sidney Bechet memorial concert; and one for an Errol Garner concert at Carnegie Hall. The two became close friends and he, as well as Louise, soon signed with Rollins and Joffe.

Woody, who was playing billiards daily then, took Cavett with him. "It was kind of fun hanging around those billiard clubs late at night. Woody had just started to appear on TV and a certain number of mug-types would come over and say, 'Hey, Woody, out playing games, ain't you?' I almost got into playing poker, too. I thought, if he's doing it, it must be the right thing to do, the way to succeed. I went to a couple of games. They were very serious. No fooling around. It was very frightening to me." On one occasion when Woody lost, though, he wrote a check to Ken Roberts, the radio announcer, that said in the memo space at the bottom, "For heart transplant."

Two years later, when Woody was performing in Los Angeles, Cavett was there writing for Jerry Lewis. The two of them sometimes walked around Beverly Hills on a Sunday morning, imagining Jack Benny and Mary Livingstone and Rochester were putting together their show for that night; they were living out the fantasies years of listening to radio shows and watching movies had instilled. Cavett also took in Woody's shows, and between sets they would look for girls. Sometimes Cavett was the only person laughing at Woody's material.

"One night, after about twelve gems in a row had gone by unrecognized by the audience who sat there blinking stupidly at the lights, he just came to a complete stop. There was an awful long moment where nobody knew if he was going to go on or what. Then he just said, 'If I were giving prizes for the worst audience I've ever seen, you'd win it.' "

Woody's hostility to the audience that night and on other occasions, such as one show at the "hungry i" when he turned his back to a rude crowd and started talking to the brick wall, showed the paradox about him: The shy Brooklyn boy who had trouble with girls, who nearly had to be led by hand to the stage when he began performing, and who covered his ears at the Bitter End if there was applause when he left the stage was also enormously self-confident about his talent.

And he was also enormously alienated from other people. Some years after their divorce, Louise Lasser said, "The worst thing in the world could happen to him and he could go in that room and write," and Woody himself once said jokingly, "I'm so alienated that I could hear my

44

parents died in a flash fire and it wouldn't affect me. I don't want to sound pretentious, but my depression is why I'm drawn to philosophy, so acutely interested in Kafka, Dostoevski, and Bergman. I think I have all the symptoms and problems that those people are occupied with: an obsession with death, an obsession with God or the lack of God, the question of why are we here. Answers are what I want. Almost all of my work is autobiographical—exaggerated but true. I'm not social. I don't get an enormous input from the rest of the world. I wish I could get out but I can't."

The theme of alienation runs through his nightclub material and his films. In *Sleeper* he plays an alien in a world two hundred years from now; in other films he is a misfit, often in another place or time against his will. His alienation is not only from people but from nature as well; one of his first jokes was, "I am two with nature." He says, "It's very important to realize that we're up against an evil, insidious, hostile universe, a hostile force. It'll make you ill and age you and kill you. And there's somebody—or something—out there who for some irrational, unexplainable reason is killing us. I'm only interested in dealing with the top man. I'm not interested in dealing with the other stuff because that's not important—although that is hard to say because there is hardly an iota of evidence of this. But the only questions of real interest are the ultimate questions, otherwise who cares about anything else?"

These feelings gave substance to his work as it developed. "People go to see you because they expect you to be a certain way. But after four or five films they suddenly say, 'that's the same old stuff.' You have to present a moving target. If you hold still long enough, someone will get you."

The fear that someone will get him operates both professionally and personally, and while probably any celebrity ought to be leery of people, Woody is more leery than most. He is genuinely shy, even afraid of people, especially strangers. If he can avoid being recognized on the street, he will. If he is stopped and there is no way out, he will graciously sign an autograph and even thank the person. But recognition does not make him comfortable in any way. Once, when he was performing in Las Vegas, he was invited by two performers to come to their show. Although he had asked their manager to make sure he was not introduced from the stage, during the last number they stopped and one said how nice it was to have Woody there. By the time the spotlight hit Woody, his face was ashen and his hands were trembling. Had there been more space or time, he would have slid under the table, which is what he started to do when he realized what was about to happen. He likes audiences because he knows they are for him, but it is not performing that he enjoys so much as having written the material or having made a film. Unlike many comedians, he does not travel with an entourage, nor is he "on" all the time. When he is not onstage or before a camera he is naturally witty in his speech but he is not in any way performing or trying to make people laugh.

While not austere—everything he buys is first class and tasteful—his life consists mainly of work. When he is not making a film, a discipline that consumes fourteen hours a day for a year, he writes much of the day. When he is making a film and there is time between camera setups,

46

he practices his clarinet or works on a piece for *The New Yorker*. During *Sleeper* he was also working on three one-act plays. He is a man of clear purpose who feels "lucky that I have some kind of gift, however minimal that gift is, and I feel dedicated to devoting my interest to it. I care only about my work, and if I can work out my interpersonal relations with a couple of people, then that's fine."

The implication of that may sound harsher than the reality, but it is fairly accurate. He is close to friends and very loyal to them, but however glad he is to see them or to be around them, they do not interfere with his work.

"Considering how obsessed he is, he was really terrific to live with," Louise Lasser says. "There was never anything fragile about his work. He gets up and goes in and writes, but you can disturb him at any time. He's not moody. He is demanding in that you pretty much have to do something when he wants. He's very specific; he won't go to any movie but a specific one. He's ritualistic about a lot of things, like the food he eats and the time he eats. [When he was filming *What's New, Pussycat?* in Paris, he ate the same dinner—soup de jour and sole—every night for six months.] He likes fish, vegetables, pie, a Hershey bar for lunch, malteds. Toy food.

"The closest we ever came to a vacation was several years ago when we went to Montauk, Long Island, for two weeks. I love being outdoors and running in the sand and he says he loves it but he avoids it. When he goes to the country to visit people he says, 'What do you do here?' For the first few days it rained, which thrilled him. Then the sun came out. The next day he woke up with sun poisoning. There was a large picture window overlooking the beach, so he sat there with this oatmeal poultice on his arms and waving. Now I know that secretly he was happy to have an excuse to sit there."

Woody's own estimation is that he's not very exciting. "I don't do any of those things one associates with masculinity. If a light switch goes out in the house I don't know where to begin to fix it. I don't drink. I don't smoke. I don't get high. My big things in life are to sit in the movies all day, to go for walks. I don't mind going to the beach for a weekend, but it's not uppermost in my mind. I'm Mr. New York City. I like to hang out with the fight mob at Madison Square Garden. If I was good enough, I could sit and play jazz all day. I think I have the type of public image where if I was caught with twelve teen-age girls in bed, or God knows what else, it would not hurt me. I think I'm a publicly avowed pervert and general scrounge. I think that people are shocked that I'm not on hash or grass."

Between 1964 and 1975, Woody wrote two Broadway plays, starring in one of them; starred in eight films, directing five of them, writing seven of them, ad libbing his part for the eighth; wrote and ad-libbed much of the dialogue for a ninth—a humorously dubbed Japanese James Bond-type film; made three comedy albums; contributed regularly to *The New Yorker;* and published two books of humorous essays. He also boxed a kangaroo in London ("A kangaroo doesn't really box. What they do is throw their arms around you and bring their two lower feet up hard, which in this country is a foul.") and sang "Little Sir Echo" on television with a talking dog. At thirty-nine, successful in every medium, he is in the rare position of being able

48

to define the terms under which he works. He is unarguably the best comic conglomerate there is and among the best in any one medium.

Critics have advanced many theories about why he is so good and why he is the right comic for our age. One critic theorizes that, as Charlie Chaplin symbolized the geographic and financial rootlessness of his era, Woody reflects the psychological and emotional rootlessness of ours. But, while theorizing has a valid place, it is not valid here. The greatest killer of comedy is dissection. Woody, as with every other original comic, never seized the idea of emotional rootlessness and said to himself, "This is how to make it." Rather, he says, "There is no conscious molding of my character whatsoever. I never say, 'Well, he wouldn't do this.' In nightclubs and films I do what I think is funny and it's one hundred percent instinctive. I just know I wouldn't shoot a guy and put him in a freezer. I just do what I do and apparently a character emerges; I have no interior judgment of the character who comes out. I can describe it only in terms of what I've heard: contemporary, neurotic, more intellectually oriented, loser, little man, doesn't get along with machines, out of place with the world—all that crap. I don't think you can try and do anything. You do it, and that's it. I'm sure there was no calculation with Chaplin even though later people would say, 'Well, the mustache represents vanity and the oversize shoes this, and the walk that.' I'm sure that what was going through his mind was, 'Hey, I bet this will be funny: I'll wear these big pants and these big shoes and this mustache and I'll look silly.' It's so accidental, so contingent. I just want to be funny. I'm not moralizing or

49

didactic in any way. And if in addition to being funny a point can be made, an inference from it, then that's all fine."

Like Chaplin and the Marx Brothers and Buster Keaton and W.C. Fields and George S. Kaufman and Robert Benchley and S.J. Perelman, Woody Allen is simply a funny man doing those things he finds funny. He is funny because he makes us laugh. And, as he would say, that is more profound than you think.

3.
"I could have made it twice as funny and half as successful."

A couple in the audience one night at the Blue Angel in 1964 was Shirley MacLaine and a man in his fifties named Charles K. Feldman, who looked a bit like Clark Gable. A conservatively dressed man in a dark suit and a quiet tie, Feldman did not laugh uproariously the way MacLaine did. What he saw when he looked at Woody was not a sophisticated comedian but rather someone who could make people laugh, and he heard not surreal, intelligent jokes, but rather a cash register ringing. Feldman was a film producer and he needed a writer to turn a frothy comedy script he had bought several years earlier for Cary Grant into a contemporary comedy that could star someone like Capucine, who happened to be Feldman's girl friend. The script had been rewritten by several other writers, one of them I.A.L. Diamond, but never in a way he liked. While MacLaine kept laughing, Feldman became convinced he had a winner in Woody. The next day he sent his emissary, a photographer-producer-graphics designer-general show business wonder named Sam Shaw, to deal with Rollins and Joffe, perhaps the only two people in show business Shaw did not know. Feldman told Shaw he could offer them up to $60,000 for Woody's services.

Shaw went to the Rollins and Joffe office, which was then one newspaper-scattered room. (They have since moved down the street to a tastefully and expensively furnished multi-large-roomed duplex with nothing scattered anywhere.) Dressed in tennis shoes, old pants, and with a bunch of newspapers under his arm, Shaw wandered into the office and went over to Joffe, who figured him for one of the crazies off the street.

"How much do you want for your boy Allen to write a movie script?" Shaw asked.

Never being one to ignore a possible good deal, even from a crazy, Joffe told him, "Thirty-five thousand dollars."

"Fair enough," Shaw said. "Feldman will be in touch with you."

A few days later Feldman was in fact in touch and they agreed that Woody would not only write the script but that he would also have a part in the film; not a bad deal for a relatively unknown twenty-eight-year-old stand-up. Feldman was right about having a winner. The film became *What's New, Pussycat?*, Feldman made millions of dollars on it, and Woody had instant, if moderate, credibility as a screenwriter and actor, even though his script was massacred by Feldman and the experience was not very enjoyable for Woody. After making three films on his own, he said of *Pussycat:* "If they had let me make it, I could have made it twice as funny and half as successful."

There were many differences between Woody and Feldman, but the most important was philosophical: Woody wanted funny, artistic successes; Feldman wanted commercial successes.

Charlie Feldman was the sort of man for whom Hollywood was invented. A lawyer-turned-agent-turned-producer, he had, according to a friend, "the soul of a gambler." As an agent he had about three hundred clients, including practically every big name: John Wayne, Gary Cooper, Richard Burton, Kirk Douglas, Greta Garbo, Marlene Dietrich, Marilyn Monroe. He did unheard-of things, like marrying Louis B. Mayer's girl friend, Jean Howard, and he made unheard-of deals: He got Irene Dunne $150,000 for one film, *Magnificent Obsession,* at a time when she had been making only $60,000 a year, and he did the same thing for Claudette Colbert for *It Happened One Night.* He raised John Wayne's fee to $750,000 plus a percentage of the profits. (Feldman claimed that he was the first agent to demand and get a percentage of the take for his stars.) He was also the first to make package deals, bringing script, star, and director (usually clients of his) to a studio which agrees to finance and distribute the film.

Among Feldman's productions were *The Glass Menagerie, The Seven Year Itch, A Streetcar Named Desire,* and *The Group.* Until his death in 1968 he had houses in, among other places, Beverly Hills, the French Riviera, New York, Rome, London, and Paris. He was called the "King Midas of Celluloid" and the "Caliph of Camp," and he was the only agent Darryl F. Zanuck would deal with when he was head of 20th Century Fox. He gave away lavish gifts to his stars (for example, he gave a $27,000 Rolls Royce to Peter Sellers after *Pussycat* was finished). He threw unbelievably lavish parties. He was the last of the big-time Hollywood producers.

Feldman was always ready to buy the person who was hot, but he was also ready to help out people who had cooled. Katherine Anne Porter needed work once and he gave her a script to work on. He had not read anything of hers until Sam Shaw had mentioned she needed work and gave him some of her stories to read. They made him break into tears and when he saw Porter he told her, "You write with your balls." She was incensed. "I write with my clitoris," she snapped.

"Charlie was generous, the kind of guy you could go to when you needed a favor," Woody says. "But he was crap to work for. Yet I have an enormous affection for him. When you see those other big-time producers, they're so cheesy and drippy. Charlie was charming and funny. He would go over to the bacarrat table and lose a hundred thousand dollars the way you'd lose your Zippo lighter. I wasn't happy with *Pussycat*. It was clearly a star vehicle. But I think small and Charlie Feldman thought big. Consequently, he was a multimillionaire when he died and I gotta work Vegas.

"He was a genius. I've seen him on one phone to Peter Sellers, on a second phone to United Artists, and on a third to the Italian government, saying, 'I can get Peter Sellers, maybe, to do this picture, I don't know,' then picking up the phone to United Artists and telling them, 'I've got to have another two hundred thousand dollars to tell Peter Sellers,' and the Italian government saying, 'You can

54

Woody Allen, 1975. (© *United Artists*)

Above: 1966. "The girls look great, but I look like a magician." (*P.I.C. Photos Ltd.*) *Below:* "This was my one good moment during the six months I was in Paris filming *Pussycat*. I was stunned that that was Samuel Beckett. He's an idol of mine. I didn't know what to say to him."

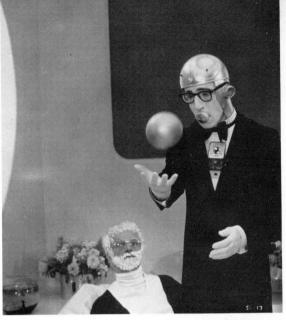

"This is a great shot, even though it didn't happen in *Sleeper*. I must say, those dummies looked great." (© *United Artists*)

In costume for the unused spider sequence in *Everything You Always Wanted to Know About Sex*. Louise Lasser is the black widow. (© *United Artists*)

Above: With Diane Keaton between shots on *Sleeper.* "This is one of the rare, rare times we've smiled while making a film." (© *United Artists*) *Below:* With Charles Joffe (left) and Jack Rollins on the set of *Everything You Always Wanted to Know About Sex.* (© *United Artists*)

1973. "My disguise hat. I wore it so much the top came off. That hat really exploded." (© *United Artists*)

With Percy Humphrey, Preservation Hall Jazz Band, 1968.

"This never made *Bananas*. We shaved 100 times, tried everything from every angle, and just *couldn't* get people to laugh at it." *(© United Artists)*

"I was 29 that day and playing my first big scene with Peter Sellers. Think I'm scared? It was so cold out that the camera froze and we had to delay shooting."

Filming *Take the Money and Run.*

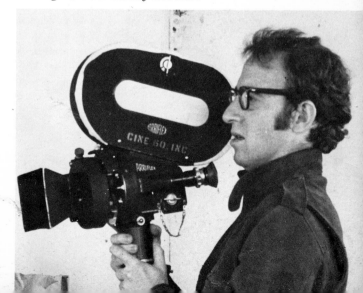

Filming *Love and Death*, 1974. The man in the vest is Fred Gallo. "This is just a funny picture." (© *United Artists*)

shoot the picture but you have to have this certain deal,' and then Sellers saying, 'I won't work in Italy,' and it went on and on. He was a big-time charming con man and I never trusted him on anything for a second. Never. He was just an out-and-out, hundred-times-over proven liar to me. I worked with him knowing that. I wish he were alive, though; not just because I wish he were alive, but I'd love him to see I was able to get into my films, because I think he would like them and because he started me."

The problem, of course, between Woody and Feldman was that Feldman would not give Woody control of his script. Not that most producers ever give a writer control. Most of them tinker with everything, and Feldman tinkered with his films as he did with everything else in his life —on a grand scale. He hired a truckload of young, talented, and innovative unknowns for *Pussycat:* Woody; Clive Donner, a director who had done only English TV; a new composer named Burt Bacharach to write the title song and a new singer named Tom Jones to sing it; Mia Fonssagrives and Vicky Tiel, two nineteen-year-old designers right out of fashion school in the U.S. but who were all the rage in Paris; and Dick Williams to do the titles— and then he didn't give his people their heads.

"He had," says Woody, "this tremendous flair for seeking out and gambling with new talent but not the sense to leave it alone so it could do its thing great. Feldman was ever present on that film: looking at dailies, looking at the script, telling me to change things, asking if he could stick in a part for one person or another. He had no regard for writers, absolutely none whatsoever. He would think nothing of hiring three writers and blending their material together. I was stunned that I was the only writer on that picture. It was such a rarity for Charlie Feldman. I don't know if it ever happened before. I think that what happened is that Charlie sensed that there was a certain kind of comedy I knew and could do and that it was hard to find other people to do it."

Feldman and Woody had trouble almost from the start. Woody was told what the Diamond script was about, but he never read it because, "I never read scripts that were given to me. I'd thumb through the first ten pages and call up and say, 'I don't think this will work and I don't want to do it.' Charlie said, 'Write something where we can all go to Paris and chase girls.' "

Woody wrote a script and read it aloud for Feldman and Warren Beatty, who was a sort of surrogate son to Feldman and who originally was supposed to star in the film. Neither liked it. "Woody couldn't quite grasp what was funny about a compulsive Don Juan," Beatty says. Woody wrote another script, very different from the first and from the script he had been given. Feldman liked it enough to go ahead with the film. Beatty found them the title. He was living at Feldman's house in Beverly Hills, always on the phone to beautiful women. His usual greeting was, "What's new, Pussycat?" Feldman, it is said, heard him once and called out, "Title!"

There are several versions of just what changes the script went through, but no matter which version, it is certain that what appeared on the screen was only remotely connected to what Woody wrote.

"In the original script," Beatty says, "Woody's part might have appeared on six pages. His first rewrite, the part went to twelve or fifteen pages and it was funny. Then it went to twenty or thirty pages. By the time we got

56

to what Woody thought was an acceptable rewrite, his part was almost half the script. Mine was almost as large but not quite as good."

Woody could write almost anything he wanted but was powerless when he tried to stick up for it. He was, in his words, "a flea compared to the others. The stars were at the zenith of their popularity and I was a total nonentity."

Feldman took Woody's script and started filling in the cast. He had astounding success. Everyone he showed the script to wanted to be in the film. It went from being a small comedy to being a big picture. Woody wanted Groucho Marx to play the part Peter Sellers was signed for. Ursula Andress, very popular then from her role in the James Bond picture *Dr. No,* got a part. Capucine, Paula Prentiss, and Romy Schneider were in. Woody went to London with Charlie Joffe to wait for filming to begin and, "When I got there I got the news—I was fiftieth to get any news—that Charlie Feldman was having trouble with Warren, that he had a commitment to another picture or something, and that Charlie was going to send the script to Peter O'Toole.

"It was one of those things of how not to make a film. We were in London for six weeks. Then Feldman thought he had a deal in Rome, so we went to Rome for six weeks. I kept insisting that the film should be made in Paris because it had a Gallic flavor, and Feldman kept saying, 'Aah, you can change it to Rome, Rome is the place.' They never had any allegiance to the script at all. We went back to Paris, then back to Rome. Months went by before the film was made, and I was shuffling back and forth, writing and rewriting. I didn't know exactly what to do. Charlie Joffe kept saying, 'Listen, you gotta roll with this because it isn't every day that a comic at the Blue Angel suddenly finds himself as the sole author and with a part in what's shaping up as the biggest comedy of the year. You have to try and see what we can get out of this rather than get temperamental and just run off.' So I was trying but it was very difficult because I was having a hard time and I had a lot of fights with Charlie Feldman about the script and whether it would be Rome or Paris.

"It was all the international set at first. I found myself having drinks with Darryl Zanuck on the Via Veneto and being taken out to dinner by Peter O'Toole. There was an enormous jet-set kind of thing, parties and boring, boring dinners in Rome or Paris that were exquisite, with three-hundred-dollar checks for dinner—wine and duck. People would start at nine o'clock and it would be finished at midnight, and I was bored stiff because I would be finished in two minutes. Charlie would just announce that we were all meeting at the Via Flavia that night, or some-place. I was in these incredible situations and always with Charlie. We would be having dinner with William Holden one night and Jules Dassin the next, and I'd be there. Capucine would call me up on a weekend and say, not romantically or anything, 'I have nothing to do, shall I take you around Paris?' It was absolutely incredible.

"Money meant nothing. We would be put up in the south of France for a week, then put up somewhere else. Then Charlie Feldman would say, 'Here, go to Florence and enjoy yourself for a week, we don't need you.' Finally, I was sightseeing with Charlie Joffe in Florence and we got a cable saying, 'Come to Paris immediately, we're going to shoot here.' And that was the beginning of it."

And only the beginning. Woody's problem and aggravation was the same with Feldman as it was with television the last few years he wrote for it: He didn't like what people were doing with his material—one of the reasons he went into performing. Now, having finally broken through as a performer, he was back in the same situation he had been in four years before when he quit television, and he resented it. Moreover, there was nothing he could do about it. He was not a film star, he was not a proven film writer, he had never directed anything, nor produced anything, either. The fact that he quite probably could have made a much funnier film, though less commercially successful, was immaterial. What mattered was that he was, as he said, a flea. And fleas can bite and irritate, but eventually they get squashed.

Feldman had a clever way to keep Woody writing good material. He'd simply tell him to write something for himself and then often give the scene to Sellers or O'Toole. But Woody's biggest complaint, other than what was done to the words, was that Feldman overproduced everything. "Everything they did was big and jazzy. They couldn't do anything small."

The plot of *What's New, Pussycat?* runs something like this: A psychiatrist named Fritz Fassbinder (Peter Sellers), whose marriage is in trouble, has a patient named Michael Jones (Peter O'Toole) who wants only to be faithful to and marry Carol Werner (Romy Schneider), his jealous-but-patient fiancée of many years whom he has been faithless to with most of the women in Europe. Three beautiful, luscious, seductive women—named Renée, Liz, and Rita (Capucine, Paula Prentiss, and Ursula Andress)—work independently to gain his favor. With the help of weakness of the flesh and such quirks of fate as, for instance, a stalled hotel elevator and a parachute being blown off course so that its attached passenger lands in his moving car, they succeed, but only momentarily. In the end, love triumphs and the marriage takes place.

There are two sub-plots. One involves Fassbinder's obsession with trying to do but once what James cannot help but do and the constant pre-coitus interruptus of his huge wife, "the creature that ate Europe." The other details the Woody Allenish stumblings of Victor Shakapopolis (Woody Allen), whose love life appears terminal before it has even begun. (Woody used the name for the character he played in the giant breast sequence of *Everything You Always Wanted to Know About Sex.*) The film featured Richard Burton in a cameo role; he walked up to O'Toole in a bar (they had just finished making *Becket* together) and said, "Don't you know me from someplace?" "It was so cute, you want to vomit," Woody says.

The pace is breakneck: Third persons stumbling into harmless interludes make them Compromising Situations; jealous wives chase wayward husbands; jealous husbands chase wayward wives; jealous lovers chase jealous lovers; would-be wayward husbands/wives/lovers are caught before the fact. There are chase scenes through apartments and streets; interrupted dramatic suicides (Sellers wraps himself in a Norwegian flag and prepares to float into the Seine in a rowboat and immolate himself Viking funeral style—the scene got the film banned in Norway); more chase scenes down country roads and through hotel rooms; a penultimate scene that gathers the whole cast at a country inn where they all run down corridors and hide in closets, cedar chests, laundry ham-

60

pers, and under beds. The final chase scene is on a go-cart track.

"It's like the Milton Berle shows without his genius, the way they produced it," Woody says. Instead of showing a normal psychiatrist's house and a normal psychiatrist's marital problems, the opening scene shows a strange castlelike art nouveau house. Seen from afar, two small figures chase each other around. Shouts are heard, bodies appear at windows, on balconies, in turrets; the camera moves to Sellers in a pageboy wig and a red velvet Little Lord Fauntleroy suit having at it with his gargantuan wife. The interior of the elevator in which O'Toole and Capucine are trapped looks better than a bridal suite. The jumpsuit Ursula Andress wears when she parachutes into O'Toole's car is made of snakeskin.

In a scene where Schneider and O'Toole declare their mutual love in dialogue purposely straight out of a bad romantic movie, Woody's script called for a small "Author's Message" to flash on and off at the bottom of the screen. "Charlie said, 'I can't flash that.' And I said, 'Well, you're wrong, because it will be just a dull, flat love scene.' Finally I got him to do it, but he fucked it up. He did it in the title design of the picture, so it's overfancy—which is what's wrong with the whole picture; it's overfancy. But it wasn't factory-made. It wasn't Doris Day."

However overproduced it was, *Pussycat* was an often funny film and it made the point Feldman was gambling on. "There's a great new audience today," he had said in the style of a great promoter. "The young adults of the world who think young, do things the young way, and live in a young manner. I make my films for a particular audience. Disney films like *Mary Poppins* are directed specifi-

61

cally to the overall family audience. My films are made for a more specific contemporary audience. They're directed toward the same people you'll find at the baseball and football games, the ones who throng to the discotheques, who wear mad fashions and keep beat to a different drummer." Fortunately, Feldman never made his living on his words, but the Pepsi generation found its filmmaker in him. In time it also found a new star in Woody Allen.

But Woody did not feel like a new star when the film was being made. If his lines weren't always given to Sellers or O'Toole, the camera was virtually always on them. When Sellers is about to commit suicide, Woody comes down to the quay and, without paying any attention to Sellers, sets up a picnic for one, complete with champagne. Upset that someone is there, Sellers asks Woody what he's doing. Woody explains that he always comes there on his birthday (it was, coincidentally, his birthday the day they filmed it). Sellers does a little slapstick and then gives up the suicide. But an even funnier scene between the two of them was passed by in favor of getting all the footage of Sellers that was possible. Woody "kept on doing the best I could. Not that I could have done better than him, he was very strong and good. But I could have contributed something."

Woody's hostility grew. "One night at rushes I told Feldman to fuck off. The Feldman contingent was there and other foreign people were hanging around. I don't know who they were. English people, French people. International money. They would be watching my gags, guys who had no relation in the world to film, and saying, 'Oh, I don't think that's funny,' or 'I think what should happen is he should be more crazy in that scene.' It's pretty hard to see rushes anyway. You work hard all day, and you're hungry, then you see your face on the screen at seven o'clock at night and you're not as funny as you thought you were. It was a nightmarish experience in many ways. I kept making nasty remarks to the point where Feldman spoke to Charlie Joffe and said, 'Can't you get your guy to stop digging me like that? It's hurting my feelings.'"

"If Woody's hurting you, you're crucifying him," Joffe told Feldman. "You're being influenced by a bunch of people who don't know anything about comedy."

Finally, about halfway through shooting, Woody and Joffe had had enough. Joffe told Feldman that Woody was through making changes and that if Feldman wanted he could take Woody's name off as screenwriter. Subsequent script changes were made by practically everyone connected with the film.

The film opened in June of 1965 to unenthusiastic, even hostile reviews. *The New York Times* said:

> Woody Allen, the nightclub comedian, is formally charged with the minor offense of having written what is alleged to be the screenplay of *What's New, Pussycat?* But Mr. Allen can deny it, if he wants to, and he is bound to be believed. He can simply state that no one in his right mind could have written this excuse for a script. . . . The idea is neurotic and unwholesome, it lacks wit, and the actors slamming through it are not true humorists.

Pussycat was booked into two New York theaters for a six-week run, but audiences loved the film and word of mouth kept them coming and packing the houses. Feldman's untapped audience was tapped. By the time the film was taken out of circulation, it had grossed $17 million, more than any other comedy ever had.

More surprising than the incredible sum of money the movie made was the attention Woody was given. People who loved the movie were happy to give him credit for the script, even though he would rather have not accepted it. People who hated it were, like the *Times*, ready to forgive and forget; they still loved him. Woody was invited on talk shows. Newspaper and magazine stories were done on him and the film. Perhaps, but not necessarily, because he was in America and the major stars were not, Woody received more exposure and publicity than anyone connected with the film, and he became its chief pitchman. "I thought that the best thing about the film was the title song," he said once on "The Tonight Show." "But it's too bad they didn't have me do it, because I wrote a terrific song." Whereupon he sang over and over, to his own horrible melody, "What's New, Pussycat? What's New, Pussycat? What's New, Pussycat?" About his own contribution, he says, "I was not in a position to tell the public, 'It isn't my fault, this is not what I would make as a picture.' It was the whole approach to filmmaking that I hate and I've since demonstrated that it isn't my kind of film. But I've never had anything as successful. *Pussycat* was just born to work. There was no way they could screw it up; try as they might, they couldn't. It was one of those things where the chemicals accidently flow right. I plugged the film on the good advice of Charlie Joffe. He felt that no matter what happened, the film was an enormous success. It was self-serving to be associated with it. In the end, it helped me from a practical point of view."

The practical point of view was that he was associated with what was then the greatest-grossing comedy of all time, and even though "the studios considered me lucky and attributed the success to everything and everyone associated with the film save me," he was still someone a studio eventually found attractive enough to finance in a film of his own. The studio was Palomar Pictures, and they put up $1.6 million for *Take the Money and Run*, having finally given in to Charles Joffe, who had insisted for a year and a half that the script (which several studios wanted to buy) would be sold only if Woody directed and starred in the film and Joffe produced it. While most film executives thought that Woody had a limited audience and was therefore a bad risk, *Take the Money and Run* and each subsequent film of the next three he wrote, directed, and starred in (*Bananas, Everything You Always Wanted to Know About Sex,* and *Sleeper*) not only earned back its money, but turned a bigger profit than the last. The four films have cost $8.7 million to produce, have grossed $36 million worldwide, and have returned a profit of about $10.5 million (*Love and Death*, the fifth film in which he has done all three, had a $2 million budget for its shooting in late 1974 and early 1975). *Play It Again, Sam,* which Woody wrote and starred in but did not direct, has grossed another $11 million.

4.
"I don't find any of this fun."

"I feel that despite what anybody says I'm a commercial comedian," Woody said one day shortly before *Sleeper* was released. He was sitting in the living room of his duplex penthouse apartment which overlooks Central Park, midtown and West Side Manhattan, having a lunch of soup and cake. The film had been shown to Los Angeles critics the night before and a little earlier in the day he had heard that Charles Champlin of the Los Angeles *Times* had liked the film a great deal; he was pleased. While Woody often says that he pays no attention to reviews, he was paying at least some to these because with *Sleeper* he was trying to move on to new ground.

"*Sleeper* is a picture every kid in America could see. It's a picture that every kid from five or six to thirteen could see and find funny. It's exactly the kind of picture that I used to see as a kid and love. It bothers me that I would be confined to intellectual humor. Chaplin had some very hip jokes in his stuff. I'm tired of being thought of as special for that Third Avenue crowd.

"I don't think I'm a special comedian. I think I've had the same problem with my movies that I had with my cabaret act in the beginning: I believe once they're in, they'll like the act or the picture. I'd like to feel that I have a broad commercial base like Chaplin, for instance—that there is a big quantitative audience. I'd like to do a series of commercially acceptable films. Instead of opening at small New York theaters like the Little Carnegie and Coronet and knowing that I'm going to break even at this figure, I want to be able to open a show the way you do a James Bond picture and get millions of people in to see it. I'd like the film to make thirty million dollars; not for me—it could all go to the cancer foundation. I just feel it's a film that there's no reason why people shouldn't enjoy it, whether they go to MIT or they're nine years old or my mother. Down through history the kind of comedy I'm doing has been very, very commercial. There's no reason for this to be like an art object or specialized thing.

"And I think I've turned the corner on *Sleeper.* I heard *Scholastic* Magazine liked it. I heard *Parents'* Magazine liked it. I'm glad about that. I heard *Seventeen* loved it and that Vincent Canby did, too."

Woody was saying this in December 1973. For the other eleven months of the year, while making *Sleeper,* he had not been nearly so sanguine. He was making the same transition as a director that he had made as a stand-up comedian—from one of the most obscure to one of the hottest—but with a very important difference: As a stand-up comedian he had absolute control over his material.

67

He wrote the jokes, rewrote them, polished and then delivered them with perfect timing. *Take the Money and Run*, his first film, was rough and uneven, primitively shot, and very funny; yet it was not so much a cohesive movie as a long visual monologue in a 35mm mosaic. But as Woody became more and more involved with filmmaking, to get the film to match his mental concepts he had to delegate more and more work to other people—set designers, cameramen, costumers—making total artistic control much more difficult. While in the end he gets his films to look the way he wants them, for a year he must deal with so many people on so many levels that filmmaking is an uncomfortable and difficult task for him.

"I got booked into some tennis doubles last weekend. I don't like it. It's a perfect example of my emotional hang-ups. I don't like doubles because I don't like being responsible to a partner. Or having a partner. I like to play singles." And filmmaking is not singles.

"I don't find any of this fun," he said one night well into the shooting of *Sleeper*. He had been on the set all day and was due at Los Angeles International Airport at midnight to make some more shots. "I face the next day with a mixture of boredom and dread. It's not fun writing a film, it's not fun shooting it, and it's not much fun editing it. There's nothing much fun involved in it. It's a compulsion to do it, because that's what I do. Thinking in terms of fun, I'd probably wind up doing a lot of those fey little things —little short stories or things like *Play It Again, Sam*, which was kind of fun to write because it dwelt on fantasies and I could write all these romantic things you could live out in real life. *Bananas* had a lot of that in it, all the

68

fantasies: running a country, getting the girl. It's got an escapist quality to it.

"Going to New Orleans to do the music will be a joy. [He played with the Preservation Hall Jazz Band recording parts of the sound track for *Sleeper*.] And what will be pleasant, if it comes to pass, is if when the film comes out and large audiences see it, they say, 'We enjoyed your film.' That's a pleasurable sensation that's hard to beat. Or to know when you're sitting at home there are thousands of people in this country or around the world sitting in movie theaters seeing your movie, and it's becoming a part of the mythology of their lives—that kids watching *Sam* and *Bananas* will grow up and will have them as a part of their conscious and unconscious forever. That's sort of a fun feeling and gratifying. And only gratifying, I guess, because I know what it meant to me when I was younger.

"I was talking with Jack Solomon [the soundman on *Sex* and *Sleeper* who has won three Oscars in his career] and he said he was the soundman on *Tom, Dick, and Harry*. And I remember in 1944 or '43—I was only eight years old —standing in front of a tailor shop in Brooklyn. They used to have these cards in the windows advertising the week's movies. And I remember seeing *Tom, Dick, and Harry* advertised and saying, 'I can't wait to see that.' It was one of those things that became a part of my conscious, because I lived in the movies and identified with that. And then here I am working with Jack Solomon and he's my soundman now. It's such a weird feeling. Twenty, thirty years ago; one of the reasons I'm in movies today is because of that.

"But to be in a film and write it and direct it is really, really hard. And I'm always worried about the money. It's always on my mind that I've got to work fast and push the crew. I make films because I have this compulsion to do it. I know I'm a screen comedian and I know that I can direct, and I do it because I do it, in the same way that I know I can write a novel and I'm going to do it. I just have to do it, I don't know why."

There may be a more compulsive and driven man around, one who is guided almost solely by a feeling of guilt if he doesn't work and a sense that he has a unique talent which he must exercise, but if he exists he has not put those drives to such variegated and successful use. Woody's life is his work. He writes because that is what he can do and likes to do, and when he says that if he were a postman he would write when he came home at night, there is every reason to believe him.

He is also a man whose confidence has increased steadily over the years, and the result of that confidence is beginning to be seen in his films.

"I think that I—I guess like everybody else—have a limited view of myself, whereas somebody outside me can alert me to a dimension that I wouldn't go to automatically. Naturally for my first movie I stayed with my safest stuff, which is stuff I know: abject humility. I was very timid in that picture. But there was no way I could have been anything else. I had never made a film, I was never the star of a picture before. When I met Pauline Kael after she saw *Take the Money and Run* she said, 'We want you to get the girl at the end. We don't want you to fail. You have a different conception of yourself.' Kael was saying that I have a masochistic view of myself, that I should

70

think of myself more as a hero and that people should identify with me because I do say funny things, from a positive way. And I believe she was right about that in the sense that I believe in *Sleeper* I came out aggressively a little bit, and I'd like to continue to do that and see what happens. I'm just beginning to feel my oats to a degree and feel more confident. I was trying to do a picture that relies more on me to get the laugh. I have to think of myself as learning all the time. I can't think that this is it, I'm finished, I'm a guy who does surreal comedy and that's all I'm going to do, I know all the ropes. I don't feel that way. I feel that over the next couple of years I should experiment with various styles of comedy."

Woody's progress as a filmmaker has been instinctive and evolutionary. Before making *Take the Money and Run* he consulted a few directors for advice, among them Arthur Penn, but "I read very little about filmmaking. I have no technical background even to this day. It's a mystique promulgated by the film industry that technical background is a big deal. You can learn about cameras and lighting in two weeks. The question is, do you want to take the time to get people who are not only very talented, but whom you can work well with, too. Film courses aren't going to do it. Someone who has something to say as a director will say it. I'm surrounded by lots of expertise in my films. I can tell those guys what I want, and then go back the next day and do it over if I have to. But you can't learn to make a film like Bertolucci in two days. It's what you say, not how you say it. If you have an unfunny film, it doesn't matter how it looks; it won't make any difference. It's common sense when you look through the camera."

When Woody is involved in one project he would usually rather be involved in another. If he is doing his stand-up act he would rather be making a film; if he is making a film he would rather be writing a play. Beyond that, self-deprecation comes easy to him along with a slightly disparaging attitude about what he does. There is a conflict in what he wants to do between comedy and drama, funny films and plays versus serious films and plays—he can do the first and wants to do the second, and the conflict makes him both more aware of the benefits and limitations of each as well as making whatever he isn't doing more attractive.

"There's no question that comedy is harder to do than serious stuff. There's no question in my mind that comedy is less valuable than serious stuff. It has less of an impact, and I think for a good reason. When comedy approaches a problem, it kids it but it doesn't resolve it. Drama works it through in a more emotionally fulfilling way. I don't want to sound brutal, but there's something immature, something second-rate in terms of satisfaction when it is compared to drama. And it will always be that way. It will never, never have the stature of *Death of a Salesman* or *Streetcar Named Desire* or *Mourning Becomes Electra*. None of it, not the best of it. If you take *School for Scandal* and *The Frogs* and *Pygmalion* and *Country Wife* and *You Can't Take It with You* and *Born Yesterday* and *Modern Times* and *Duck Soup,* and that's much of the best of the crop you're talking about, they'll never have the impact of *The Seventh Seal* and *Potemkin* and *Greed* and whatever because there's something less satisfying about comedy, even though it is harder to do. The problem is, when you're doing a comedy it's okay to worry about photography, but relentlessly coming up on your tail at all times is that monster that you've got to be fast and funny, you've got to be relentlessly funny. I don't mean a joke every second. You could be doing a comedy that had a joke every five minutes, and not a gag but character humor, but you've got to keep the rhythm going or the ground rules you laid down in the first five minutes, the deal you made with the audience to be fast and funny, are violated. And because of that it's very, very difficult and frequently just impossible to do the kind of things that are interesting to me, certainly, and to probably other people in films.

"What's interesting to do is some of the other more schmaltzy kinds of stuff. All the schmaltzy kinds of things you can do with film are done by Bergman and Antonioni. Great mood stuff. Serious directors have the most fun. *Cries and Whispers* has lots of close-ups, and the color is printed down. That's not appropriate for comedy. The good-looking stuff is the stuff without laughs in it. That's why the most fun I've had with anything was the Italian sequence in *Everything You Always Wanted to Know About Sex*, because I could just come in and not think about anything except what is the fanciest, the best shot I can make with the camera. I didn't have to worry if it's dark, or if it's moody, or if someone's half-shadowed or half-blocked, because it contributes to the joke—I'm satirizing the style of shooting. It was such a pleasure. And when I was getting ready to make the film I wasn't even going to include that sequence in it until Louise came over to my house for dinner one night. We had already gone to Palm Springs and picked out the desert location for the sequence on masturbation that we were going to

73

do. Louise was going to play Onan's wife and I was going to be Onan. She was reading through the script and saw the Italian sequence and I said, 'Yeah, it's out.' And she said, 'I think it's great. I think it's much more funny and stylish than what you have in there.' And we started to talk. I saw the thing shot in peasant style, totally. I saw it done in the Vittorio de Sica style. It never occurred to me to do it as a contemporary Italian film. The premise of the thing seems to be of a guy in a small village—his wife can't have an orgasm, and they ask a guy in the church—it would never be done today. I saw it strictly as peasants in a little Sicilian village, and it would be shot in that black-and-white style of *Open City* and *The Bicycle Thief,* that sort of thing. Then she said, 'No, no. I hear footsteps in a large corridor and I see Ferraris and that kind of thing.' And I said, 'You're crazy, it can't work like that, because those kind of people wouldn't have that problem and they wouldn't consult a priest.'

"We argued and argued. Then I said, 'Let me think.' And I tried to get Paula Prentiss and Richard Benjamin to play it, and I tried to get John Cassavetes and Raquel Welch to play it, and those people and others turned it down. Finally I decided I'd play it with Louise. And then I began to see it; I had more and more ideas. I really started to feel that piece. I just love it. Some of the shots in there are dynamite. The shot right after I pull away from the wedding and she's by the Venetian blinds in the apartment waiting for me—it's great. The color is great. It looks like a totally satirical Bertolucci shot. It's dark and there is a vase with some purple flowers and the slats are on the windows and the light's coming through. Some of it is knockout. Some of it is not as knockout.

"It would take us three hours to do one of those shots, but I never had anything to do except worry about imitating one of those styles. If I did one of those shots in *Sleeper*, if Miles Monroe is talking with Dr. Tryon and the camera goes behind the light and Miles is framed between two leaves of a tree, it's no good. A good example is Mike Nichols's direction of a play on Broadway: simple, fast, clean, light, perfect. And the directions work. And Kazan's direction, something like *J.B.*, with the area lighting and pinspots, is what's fun to do but what would murder comedy.

"When it comes down to survival, it's laughs that a comedy has to have. There's no way out of it. There's a route that everybody in the world who does comedy takes to try to get around that because laughs are so hard to get. It's not hard to get one or two, but it's hard to get ninety minutes of laughter at a quick enough pace that people aren't bored. It's so difficult that you try everything else. Guys are always saying that what you want to have are some interesting characters so that they go with the story. And yes, of course, you definitely want them, all that's wonderful—if the laughs are there. But if the laughs aren't there, then all that stuff just doesn't mean anything. Whereas if all that stuff's not there but the laughs are, then you've got a good chance for a winner. In the end it's just a pragmatic thing that laughs are the heart and blood of a comedy.

"The thing to remember about *Play It Again, Sam* is that it is filled with laughs. All the character business and all that plot involvement would have meant nothing if it didn't have an enormous amount of laughs. Also, it was a play, so with a play you write characters. *Sam* was a play

75

made into a film that will always be a good story—though a trifle—a good kind of film that long after I'm dead people will be able to curl up in bed and watch on TV and always like and say, 'Oh, that's a cute kind of story from the sixties,' and that kind of thing, just as we watch *It Happened One Night* or those kinds of films now. Less interesting to watch at home, say, is *Modern Times*, or Buster Keaton, because that's a different genre.

"The kind of films I make, with the exception of *Sam*, and the kind of films Chaplin and the Marx Brothers made are not the kind of films good for television or for home showing. I think you want to go out to a crowded theater; there's a lot of tension there and it's a group experience. When you see them at home, they don't hold your interest. I could see *Duck Soup* anytime more than *It Happened One Night*. But when I'm home in bed watching television, I need a story. The story becomes very important. Alfred Hitchcock mentioned this to me once. I was asking him the difference between his television show and his films, and he said story is everything on television.

"The films that I'm making are much more indigenous to film than they are to the stage. *Sleeper* and the sex film are basically where I'm working as a comedian who could only be me. I have to be the comedian of *Sleeper*. What the film is about is a comedian, just like Groucho's films are about Groucho Marx. *Duck Soup* is not a script that you can hire actors to play. What makes *Sleeper* funny is me, if I do make it funny. Whereas the play *Play It Again, Sam* is a completely different experience. That I wrote and it's been played successfully by other people and might have been played better than by me. It's much more conventional and it's a different taste. It's a more popular taste. On the other hand, people have said to me, 'Don't ever make that kind of film again—it's not your kind of film.' After *Sam* I got letters from people saying, 'Well, it looks like you've sold out now.' But I wouldn't hesitate, despite what anybody said, to make another film like *Sam*. I want to mix it up. That was one experience. I don't think a person should make a single kind of film. I think that's a mistake."

In order to avoid making that mistake, Woody wanted *Sleeper* to be something new for him—a movie that required more than ever his individual talents as a comedian to make the film work.

"Jokes become a vehicle for the person to display a personality or an attitude," Woody says often and in different ways. "Just like Bob Hope. You're not laughing at the jokes but at a guy who's vain and cowardly and says to some guy who is menacing, 'You're looking good—what do you hear from your embalmer?' You're laughing at character all the time. There's no question that all comedians play off basically overlapping things. I could say Hope, Benny, Chaplin, Keaton, Groucho, and I all like women; we're all cowardly—Groucho will be menaced by the face of a gangster and he'll be hiding in the closet on board ship. We're all playing off the same things: vanity, cowardice, lust for women, lust for importance. I think all comedians overlap that way. The kind that never make it are the kind that come out on television and say, 'Take my kid brother. He's always watching television. We didn't know he walked until he got up.' That kind of stuff. No person emerges."

In order to make a person emerge in his character in

Sleeper, Woody took risks that he had avoided in his earlier films. In *Take the Money and Run* and *Bananas* especially, his character depended largely on material and jokes Woody brought to the film as a writer. In *Take the Money and Run*, for instance, two of the funniest sequences are dependent almost exclusively on their concepts and not on how they are acted. In one, bank robber Virgil Starkwell (Woody) goes into a bank and gives the teller a hold-up note.

TELLER
What does this say?

VIRGIL
Uh . . . can't you read it?

TELLER
Uh . . . I can't read this. What's this
. . . "act natural"?

VIRGIL
No, it says, "Please put fifty thousand
dollars into this bag and act natural."

TELLER
It does say "act natural"!

VIRGIL
(looking at note) Uh . . . "I am pointing
a gun at you."

TELLER
That looks like gub, that doesn't look
like gun.

VIRGIL
(studying note with teller) No, that
. . . that's gun.

TELLER

Uh . . . no, that's gub . . . that's a "b".

VIRGIL

No . . . that's an "n" . . . that's . . . uh
. . . gun.

TELLER

(signaling to another teller) Uh . . .
George, would you step over here a
moment please? . . . What does this
say?

GEORGE

"Please put fifty thousand dollars into
this bag and abt natural." What's
"abt"?

VIRGIL

"Act"!

TELLER

Does this . . . does this look like "gub"
or "gun"?

GEORGE

"Gun," see? But what's "abt" mean?

VIRGIL

"Act." That's "act natural." It says,
"Please put fifty thousand dollars into
this bag and act natural."

TELLER

Oh, I see . . . this is a hold-up.

VIRGIL

Yes.

TELLER

May I see your gun?

79

VIRGIL

Oh. (*reaching under jacket and lifting
gun in his belt partially up*)

TELLER

Well, you'll have to have this note ini-
tialed by one of our vice-presidents
before I can give you any money.

VIRGIL

Please, I'm in a rush.

TELLER

I'm sorry, but that's our policy . . . the
gentleman in the gray suit.

Virgil goes to the vice-president and the same argument ensues. By the end, everyone in the bank is involved
with trying to decipher the note.

Earlier in the film, Virgil is shown in prison, where he
is serving time for robbing an armored car—with a stolen
gun that turned out to be a cigarette lighter. Virgil almost
succeeds in an attempted escape with a gun carved out of
a bar of soap and colored with black shoe polish, but unfortunately it rains heavily the night he tries and by the
time he gets across the prison yard and to the gate with
his guard hostages, all that's left of the gun is a handful of
suds. Two more years are added to Virgil's sentence, but
one day a new opportunity arises.

WARDEN

We need some volunteers for an experiment. The doctors want someone
innoculated with a new vaccine. . . .
It's never been tried on humans
before, so we don't know what the side

80

effects may be. To be honest, you'll be taking a chance. As a reward, there's a parole. . . . I am sure some among you are brave enough to take the risk.

NARRATOR

With parole as an inducement, Virgil submits to the vaccine test. It is a success, except for one temporary side effect. For several hours he is turned into a rabbi.

VIRGIL

(in cell with beard and rabbi's vestments on) And so the reason we celebrate the Passover holidays by eating the matzos is to commemorate the time when Moses led the Children of Israel from Egypt.

While visually funny, those are the jokes of a writer in a room, not of a film comedian. They are funny because they were written funny and anyone could get a laugh with them. A comedian gets laughs by virtue of his character and particular talents. Woody wanted *Sleeper* to have everything in it: a plot as well as visual comedy, good photography, and many of the advantages of the silent comedies—jokes that relied solely on the comedian without need of words.

The idea for the film occurred to him while he was making *Everything You Always Wanted to Know About Sex*. He and Fred Gallo, his first assistant director, were driving to the set one day and Woody said to Gallo, "I have an idea for a picture. How much do you think it would cost to build a futuristic town?"

"Millions," Gallo replied.

"There are four things to stay away from in movies," Gallo said one night when *Sleeper* was about three-quarters done and a month behind schedule. "Boats and water; animals; kids; and futurism."

Woody, however, pays no attention to injunctions that interfere with an idea that he likes, and he liked the idea of *Sleeper:* Miles Monroe, who runs the Happy Carrot health food store, goes into a hospital in 1973 for a routine operation. Complications set in, he never regains consciousness, he is cryogenically frozen, and 200 years later he is defrosted by a political underground group.

Woody called Marshall Brickman, a friend who had started as a folk singer in the early sixties, became head writer for Johnny Carson, and was, in the summer of 1972 when Woody called him, producer and creative director for Dick Cavett. He asked him if he wanted to help write the script. They had collaborated five years earlier on a script entitled *The Filmmaker.* But "no one else thought it was funny," Brickman says, and the film was never made.

During the late summer and early fall of 1972, Brickman and Woody walked in Central Park, looked at girls, talked about the movie and other things, and went to each other's apartments to work on the script. In about six weeks they had a first draft with a lot of dead ends in it, but one that also had gotten rid of several others, among them ideas that demanded too much suspension of disbelief on the part of the audience. For instance, there were to be two time capsules at the beginning—one with Woody inside, the other containing someone like Burt Lancaster or George C. Scott. Woody would marvel at

82

being in this strange predicament with a screen hero who was now just himself; and then instead of the star, Woody would turn out to be the hero. They also considered—and discarded—the idea of making an intermission film with the first half taking place in the present and the second half in the future.

Woody and Marshall make an interesting contrast. Brickman analyzes things and asks if they're plausible or believable, and Woody simply says, "Yes, but is it funny? You may be right, but if they don't laugh, where are you?"

"I suggest taking out a joke for structure and Woody looks at me as though I've spilled ink on the carpet," Brickman says. "But it's only the best fun working with Woody. He's instructive, hilarious, interesting. He's very gentlemanly and there are never any arguments. Generally, one person is clearly right. Woody has the determination to sit and get the line right; he has faith in his own instincts.

"Woody and I wrote *The Filmmaker* when he was acting on Broadway in *Play It Again, Sam.* He called me up and said he had a couple of ideas for a film and did I want to do one? I was head writer for Carson at the time so I was busy all day, and the trouble was that the only time we could meet was after his show got out, about ten-thirty.

So we would go to Sardi's or Woody's and talk until one or one-thirty, which should give you some idea about Woody's dedication, or obsession. But those hours may be why *The Filmmaker* was so fragmented. So for *Sleeper* I took a sabbatical from the Cavett show and we talked like humans during the day."

In the fall of 1972 they finished a draft suitable to

83

show to David Picker, then president of United Artists. Woody's deal with UA allows him the freedom all directors dream of but few ever get: He has absolute control over everything—script, casting, and final cut. And the way the deal was made was as simple as any screenwriter could fabricate. It was arranged by Charles Joffe and Picker under the grandstand in Madison Square Garden at a rally for John Lindsay in 1969. At that time, Woody had directed only *Take the Money and Run*, but Picker was interested in having him do films for UA (United Artists had already blown one opportunity with Woody. They offered only $750,000 as a budget for *Take the Money and Run*, which Rollins and Joffe turned down. "It would have killed the script," Joffe says.) When Picker and Joffe accidentally ran into each other at the rally, Picker asked Joffe what kind of deal Woody wanted to come to UA and Joffe told him, "Two million budget, total control after you approve the story idea, and a three-film contract."

"Fine," Picker said. "Get your lawyers on it." And they shook hands in agreement.

The only addition to the agreement was that if a film went over budget, Woody and Rollins and Joffe would cover the excess out of their fees: $350,000 for Woody as writer, director, and star; $150,000 to Rollins and Joffe as producers. (In addition, Woody has $200,000 and Rollins and Joffe have $50,000 deferred. They are paid that as soon as the film recovers its cost—generally 2.7 times the actual production cost. There is no profit distribution until they receive their deferments.) If the excess was more than the fees, UA would cover the remainder. If the film turned a profit, they would then recover their fees.

84

Sleeper is the only film to have gone over budget. Even so, at a final cost of $3,100,000, *Sleeper* was by far the least expensive major film released for the 1973 Christmas season. *The Sting*, for instance, cost about $8,000,000, *Day of the Dolphin* about $9,000,000, and *The Exorcist* about $12,000,000.

Picker liked the script for *Sleeper* and approved it even though it was different from other scripts Woody had brought in. It is not a very funny script to read. By intent, there are fewer jokes that are simply the product of a funny writer and more jokes that rely on the ability of the comedian to carry them off. When Woody asked Picker if he thought it was a funny script, he said, "Not particularly. There are block comedy sequences that depend on execution, but I trust you to do it. If anyone had come in with Chaplin's conveyor belt scene from *Modern Times* it wouldn't have read as much, either. Both scripts depend on the comedian."

"I feel less secure with *Sleeper* than I have with any of my films going into it, because I do feel that the film has to happen at the time," Woody said before leaving New York for Los Angeles, where he would make a good part of the movie. "This is a physically hard and dangerous film, but it's necessary for a slapstick-type of picture, just as improvisation is necessary; and I think if a person's funny, he can be funny verbally as well as physically. I've tried to make a marriage here of good verbal gags and a decent relationship with the girl and a nice novel setting and plenty of jokes. It will be interesting to see when we edit it if the relationship will take over or if it will be basically a slapstick film or if all of it will work."

85

5.
"We need one with a little more gorgiositude."

As in any specialized field, filmmaking has its own argot. MOS is Katzenjammer Kids English (mitout sound) for silent filming; dailies, or rushes, are the developed scenes shot the day before and viewed by the director to see if they need to be redone; wrap means the end of a day's work; a gaffer is an electrician. For men there is a cowboy close-up (from the six-guns on up); for women, a Montana close-up (just above the Buttes). While most terms define specifics, a few are catchalls. Preproduction is a catchall which encompasses what happens over the period of months before shooting begins when the producer and director plan how and where to spend, they hope, a little less than their budget allows. It is a process that includes arranging for virtually everything that will be needed for a film. Stars must be chosen; supporting actors and bit players must be picked with the help of a casting agency;

shooting locations must be arranged for; sets must be designed and built; a crew must be found; the script must be
broken down into a schedule of what scenes will be shot
where, and when, and in what order; props must be
chosen and in some cases designed and tested; in short, by
the day shooting begins, everything and everyone necessary to make the film should have been found, bought,
hired, and arranged for, so that the film can be shot according to some sort of rational plan and schedule. That
seldom happens in Woody's films, but everyone tries.

In February 1973 Woody began preproduction on
Sleeper. He had two and a half months before shooting
began; he could have used six.

Given a choice, which to a large degree he now has and
is exercising, Woody would always rather work with
someone he knows and trusts—as would anyone, for that
matter. To that end he is building a more or less permanent crew and group of major actors. Even so, unless he
has something to say, Woody's comments to practically
everyone in the planning of a film or on the set are kept
to a minimum, as they are in his life to anyone who isn't
a good friend. Part of the reason for his reticence is his
shyness; part of it is because he simply does not like to
have much to do with many people and he is in a position
where he does not have to. Though he is seldom overtly
rude, his silence and detachment can be disconcerting.
Although recently he has begun to open up more, he does
not recall ever interviewing alone someone up for a major
spot in the cast or crew, "because I find it hard to encounter a person. I can't really learn about them if I do it alone
because my head is swimming at the time," so a third
person generally asks the questions while Woody sits qui-

etly and listens. He sat quietly and listened often in the planning of *Sleeper* (although he ultimately made every major decision and many of the small ones). One day he was trying to select an actor to play The Leader, a character whose picture abounded in the film but who had no lines. Woody received each candidate in his bungalow on the lot.

The lot was the old Culver City Studios in Los Angeles, where *Gone with the Wind* and *Duel in the Sun*, among hundreds of other movies, were shot. Woody's bungalow, which normally served as a star's dressing room but occasionally was used in exterior shots, looked from the outside like the residence of a small, lower-middle-income family. Some daisies grew in front, there was a foot-high white picket fence around the flower bed, and a name-and-address stake put there for some forgotten film leaned out through the flowers. Inside there was a kitchen, a small room with a desk, and two larger rooms, one filled mainly by a pool table, and the other furnished with a couch, a record player for Woody's jazz records, and a Movieola. Clark Gable used the bungalow, with different furnishings, as his dressing room for *Gone with the Wind*.

Woody sat on the edge of the pool table and watched while Elizabeth Claman, his secretary for the film, greeted each prospect by the desk. She made sure each name was the same as the list said it should be and asked how tall they were. Each looked puzzled but answered.

"Thank you, that's all," she said to each.

"That's all?" several asked, sometimes peering in at Woody.

After an actor left, Woody told Elizabeth whether he thought he might be good for either the part of The Leader or some other part, but he fell into the problem of liking each one better than the last.

"It's like the Marx Brothers," he said, crossing yet another name off the list the way Groucho and Chico ripped up a contract clause by clause in *A Night at the Opera*. "We need one with a little more gorgiositude, but not too much." (Adding "iositude" to the end of adjectives is an old trick of Woody's and an easy way to spot his contribution to a collaborative script in his TV-writing days. He picked up the habit twenty years ago, he says, when he saw a book entitled *The Essence of Negritude*. "It was a serious book, but I thought the title was funny.")

After musing awhile about who should do what, he shook his head. "Fellini just pulls them off the street," he said to no one in particular, and looked up to see what the next man looked like.

A few days after the cast had been chosen, he had a rehearsal of those who would play the doctors in the underground movement. Since Woody worries that the plot of a new film will become known before the film is released, he gives actors only pages of their own dialogue; only those who absolutely must have whole scripts get them.

So the actors were gathered around the pool table with their pages of dialogue, which were from an earlier version of the script than Woody had. Woody assured them that they would be given the changes but that they would know what they needed to know about their scenes from what they had. The actors, naturally enough, were curious to learn as much about their parts as possible. Woody answered their questions but gave away very little of the whole story.

"The picture is satirical of now," he told them, "even though it takes place two hundred years from now. We don't want to make these characters too omnipotent. They are good people, people like you are today."

At one point they came to a scene in which one doctor says there has been a war and explains to Woody what has happened to civilization as he knew it: "According to history, over a hundred years ago a man by the name of Albert Shanker got hold of a nuclear warhead." They asked what it meant, because Albert Shanker, a strident man who is head of the United Federation of Teachers in New York City, is not generally known outside the state.

"There are several jokes we're going to try here," Woody told them, "because I want to give myself some alternatives." (Included in the alternatives to the Albert Shanker reference were: "some New York taxi drivers" and "an organization called the D.A.R." The Shanker reference was finally used in the film, much to the roaring approval of New Yorkers and to the mystification of the rest of the country. Woody has no qualms about using a parochial joke if it pleases him more than any other that might be used in a certain spot.)

As Woody explained what he wanted to do, he never assumed any of the actors had seen any of his other films, and he always explained the references he made to them. He and the actors went through the scene a few times.

"I'd like to read the scene one more time, if that's all right," he said to them. "I want to play everything as realistically as possible and—I'll forget this, I know—keep it going at a good clip."

"Ambivalence is the death of comedy," Woody said after the actors had left. "In silent-film style they are cartoon characters: they fight one another and the next frame they're up and okay. Actors want to complicate characters, give them ambivalent relationships. You want to look at a character and immediately know, that's a good man, or a bad man. Chaplin's style was to play against other characters. You see him coming down the street swinging his stick and you know immediately what's going to happen."

In filmmaking, unfortunately, there is very little that you immediately know will happen. What looks good during filming often doesn't, for some mystical reason, look good on film. And what may look good on film by itself often looks terrible when cut into sequence. So for *Sleeper* Woody worked out several slapstick routines and spent a good deal of time inventing a walk that would make him look like a robot. The walk was very hard to develop. Over a period of days, whenever he had a moment, he practiced it and varied it. Finally he decided to film a few sample walks in black and white and see how they looked on the screen.

"I can walk wry," he said after trying a walk that made those watching him laugh. "Specializing in puckish walks." He tried another version. "I can't believe a man of my intelligence has to walk funny to make people laugh."

After the filming, he walked over to the sound stages to see a set while talking about the revisions he still wanted to make in the script and how he viewed himself primarily as a writer. "In writing, the introverted part of self takes over. Producers, directors, actors are more aggressive. Writers can be taken advantage of. Writing can be so hard. There are times writers will do anything to avoid writing—take a job as a director or actor, for instance."

Doing the director's job of going off to look at locations is something Woody does usually only under duress, and he will put it off or avoid it in any way he can until the last minute—often to the dismay of Fred Gallo, or Dale Hennesy, the set designer, because each of them needs to know Woody's decision as much in advance of shooting as possible.

One Saturday morning shortly before shooting was scheduled to begin, there were no other outs available and he had to fly from Los Angeles to Monterey at 8:30 A.M. to spend the day looking over three possible sites. He had gone to Monterey a couple of weeks earlier, but nothing looked good to him. So the locations man had come up with some other choices. One of the issues at stake was how much shooting could be done in Monterey, how much in Denver, and how much on the set.

Woody is not a good traveler. "I don't like plane flights," he said as the plane went through an air pocket. "I hate riding in a car, for that matter. When I consider it, I dislike the wheel."

Once on the ground he wasn't much happier, and he muttered a lot about finding a Sambo's (a chain of restaurants in California similar to Howard Johnson's). "I don't want to be pressed into making a decision on an empty stomach," he complained, but no Sambo's was to be found and there wasn't time to eat anyway.

Driving up the coast by fields and fields of artichokes, Woody was quiet, though Gallo and Hennesy tried to cheer him up. In a while the car came into Castroville, the self-proclaimed "Artichoke Capital of the World," according to a banner hung across the street. Woody picked up a bit. "This whole town is about artichokes," he marveled. "I wonder what the mayor wears? There's the bank. They all come in and deposit their artichokes."

After a few minutes he started talking about how funny it would be to have a giant artichoke in a scene where Miles Monroe (Woody) comes across a garden full of gargantuan vegetables. For the past few weeks Hennesy's crew had been building a twelve-foot-high celery bush, a three-foot-high strawberry, and an eight-foot-long banana, all of which looked alarmingly real. The prospect of coming up with a monstrous artichoke in short order made Hennesy wince. After a while the countryside began to look a little like Long Island. Woody liked that more.

One of the sites to be checked out was down a dirt road that opened onto a grassy bluff which dropped a hundred feet to the Pacific. The grass was perhaps eighteen inches high, and Woody, who does not like dealing with nature, hated having to walk around in it. He was uncomfortable until he got back on the dirt road, where he decided that the site would not work.

"I'm not up for this film yet," he said in partial explanation of his general unhappiness. "It's a little like a prize fighter who has to get up for a title bout. A tremendous amount of energy is spent on each film in finding places that look like Puerto Rico [*Bananas*] or Italy [for a sequence in *Sex*] or the future [*Sleeper*]. *Play It Again, Sam* was nice that way because we could just walk a guy down the street."

The problems in finding places that looked appropriate seemed endless. Woody did not want to use fabricated sets except when absolutely necessary, so massive logistic procedures were needed to move cast and crew over most of California and a good portion of Colorado. Although there had once been serious talk of shooting in Brasilia, it was ruled out because of expense and the general problems of shooting in Brazil. Colorado was chosen as a location because Woody saw a house in an architecture magazine that looked just like what he wanted, and because it seemed that with a limited amount of set shooting for interiors, almost everything could be done in Denver, Boulder, and the nearby Rockies.

In addition to the house, which looked like a hamburger with a side sliced off it sitting on a pedestal, Denver also had a number of other buildings that could be used for several different scenes. Not only did *Sleeper's* buildings have to look futuristic, the landscape had to have a timeless quality to it. Even though shooting took place in the Rockies and on the Mojave Desert and in rolling hills above the sea at Monterey, most of the scenery finally looked generally indistinguishable. (It is not possible, for example, to tell that one scene where Woody is wearing a flying pack and being chased by police was shot over a period of four months—some of it in the spring in Colorado, some there in late summer, and even a close-up or two done in California.)

Woody's concern for how a shot looks showed up strongly for the first time during the filming of *Everything You Always Wanted to Know About Sex*. *Sex* was cinematographer David Walsh's first film with Woody. As he tells it, "A friend said, 'David, why would you want to do a film with Woody Allen? His films look awful.' I had seen him on TV and thought he was a clever guy, but I had never seen one of his films. Then I saw *Bananas*. I didn't know what to say or do after seeing it. It was not what I know or what I want to do. But when I was hired, I was told, but not by Woody, 'If you like being in charge, it's good, because you'll be making all the technical decisions.' Then suddenly Woody starts asking not technical questions but questions that require a technical answer, like why the camera should go in a certain place. He was interested in finding out. There were no haphazard circumstances in any regard."

"On my first two films I was intimidated—I was fighting for survival," Woody says. "I wanted them to be funny and all my effort went into that. In *Sex* I started to come out of myself a little more. I wanted to make a funny picture that looked interesting."

Woody's change in attitude was not at all gradual. He saw the rushes of the first day's shooting on *Sex* and decided that they did not look the way he wanted. From then on, to the surprise of everyone who had worked with him before, he began paying a great deal of attention to how the scenes were shot. His change meant that for the first time he was having sets rebuilt if necessary and that he was less concerned with staying on schedule. Keeping the picture within its budget required all of producer Jack Grossberg's and Dale Hennesy's ingenuity—Grossberg because he controlled the money and Hennesy because he had to build sets within the money allotted.

For Woody *Sex* was a necessary step toward integrating humor with pretty shots, and he knew that he would be sacrificing some laughs and spending more time and money than he had before to get the look he wanted.

"We overcovered a lot in *Sex*," Walsh recalls. "Who knows what's going to work, because Woody says he thinks he knows what *might* work? So you're foolish not to try that as well. I once worked with [film director] Henry Hathaway. Hathaway was predictable. He would give you a list in the car of eight shots and how to shoot each one. He usually had a big cigar in his mouth and he would often say, 'One thing I can do is make a fucking decision. I won't be right all the time but I'll be right most of the time.' If Woody has a problem, it's getting himself to prepare. Sometimes you have to get him to make decisions in advance. Freddy and I took him to the vegetable patch [with the gargantuan celery and banana and strawberry]. By the time we got to shooting it, it was completely different than he had conceived it, but we were ready because we had gotten him to talk about it. Then he said, 'Now I need new gags.'

"I've worked with John Frankenheimer, Stuart Rosenbloom, Stanley Kramer, Sam Peckinpah, and Roman Polanski, as well as Hathaway. All of them have separate spots, all of them are different. Woody will find a frame that's really a classic and has a lot of merit to it that some cameramen and artists couldn't find in a lifetime."

Woody's relationship with Walsh developed steadily during the filming of *Sex*. Now Walsh, like Gallo, has become one of the people Woody relies on for each film he makes, and he has started giving them part of his profit as well as their salaries.

About half of the rest of the crew for *Sleeper* had worked with Woody on *Sex*. Jack Grossberg, who maneuvers budgets in ways that would impress a Zurich gnome ("You could wake Jack up at three in the morning and he'd try to beat you out of a few dollars," Woody says.), had somehow managed to bring in *Bananas* and *Sex*, the two films he has produced, on budget. There was no way, though, that *Sleeper* was going to come in on the money, and within the first few weeks of shooting that was clear to everyone.

"When we began *Sleeper*," Gallo said one night, "Woody thought *Sex* was a harder picture. You could have *phoned Sex* in in comparison to this. Jack, anybody, would have to have a direct line to God to get this one in on budget."

Grossberg, however, is the one man who has been with Woody from the start (he was production manager on *Take the Money and Run*) who, for now anyway, will be doing no more projects with him. As Woody has developed his filmmaking talents and ideas and gained confidence in himself, he has come to need less and less the services of a producer, whose job it is to arrange the talent and crew and keep the film on budget and on time. Since Woody has ultimate control of his films (producers normally do), and since he is willing to take extra time and spend extra money to get the film he wants, he has become de facto producer of his movies. Grossberg, meanwhile, whose first job as a producer was with Woody, has grown in talent and stature in his field and wants simply to be a producer, and working with Woody is going to be at best frustrating.

"He's a genius, I love him," Grossberg says of Woody, "but his concepts of what happens to prepare something are nil. He finds his locations only under protest. My job is to make sure the respective people perform. I can interpret his fantasies into reality; I can get the things and put the people together. Since everything is subservient to the joke, he is willing to compromise the set, the costumes, the location just for the sake of the joke. Funny is money, as Jack Rollins says. But he's really been an experience for me. He's really professional. He offers up more excitement to me than anyone else. Being associated with his project is more important than the money. Usually in this business guys are at each other's throats after one or two pictures trying to cut up the booty. It's never been like that with Woody. He has no concept of money—as long as he can put his hand in his pocket and take out whatever he wants. I bet if you ask him how much money he was getting for this picture, he wouldn't know." (Apparently, he didn't.)

It is Grossberg who plays the heavy in the film company. He's the one who hires, fires, and says no as often as possible. He's also the man in the middle, having to deal with crew problems while adjusting to Woody's needs and providing what he wants. ("It's your fantasy," he said with a shrug to Woody when he asked one day if Jack could work out the details so that another four days could be spent shooting a scene.) Because Woody frequently changes his mind about sets and shots, and shooting on the film always lasts longer than it is supposed to, Grossberg works hard at keeping the crew as happy as he can while driving them as hard as he can; working weekends and evenings, for instance. He is not above co-opting them whenever possible and does things like putting a bottle of Scotch in each person's room when they go on location.

"The crew always comes in after a couple of weeks, complaining about the workload or the expense money or something," Grossberg said one night after the crew had come in complaining about the workload and the expense money and something else. "I assure them we're not going to destroy them."

Fred Gallo is the most important person in Woody's crew, as evidenced by his being the only one Woody took to France to film *Love and Death* when it became clear that taking an American crew there would be prohibitively expensive. He has worked on all of Woody's films and never takes a job with someone else without checking first with Woody to see if he needs him during that time. He keeps everything moving on the set, he handles the cast and crew, he calls for action on each shot (usually the director does) and says when to cut after Woody turns and says, "Okay?" ("I think shouting 'Action!' sounds corny," Woody says. "I just can't see myself going on a set and yelling 'Action!' "), and he sets the daily shooting schedule. Beyond that, he has the ability to carry out all of what Woody wants and to anticipate most of his needs. On *Sex* he drove Woody to the set so he could explain what scenes they were going to shoot that day. Since *Take the Money and Run* someone has always driven Woody to the set.

"Woody drove his own car in San Francsico for *Take the Money*," Gallo recalls. "It was a red Mustang convertible. One day he is more or less driving well with me and the cop assigned to the picture in the car, and he says, 'I've got to get a license.' And everybody laughs until we realize he's not joking. So we go and he takes the tests. Then every night I would tell him where the next day's location was, but he would only manage to get near it. So we had two motorcycle cops on lookout for a red car, and we'd see him going up the block, then past the park where we were, and they'd take off and bring him in."

Grossberg hired Gallo to work on *Take the Money*. The two of them had worked on Mel Brooks's film *The Producers*—Grossberg as unit manager and Gallo as a coordinator for the dancers ("I'm back from Vietnam three days and here are all those girls with pretzels on their boobs.").

A few months later Grossberg was lining up the crew for *Take the Money*. "Jack needed a unit manager, so he called me and said he was going to San Francisco and did I want the job? We haggled on price and I worked my way up to scale."

By the time *Bananas* came along, Gallo had become first assistant director and was making much better than scale (although he says, and has demonstrated by doing it on an abortive National Educational Television special Woody made in 1971 for PBS, that "Woody is the only guy I'd work scale with."). While Gallo and Woody have a strong and mutual respect and a fine working relationship, they see virtually nothing of each other between films.

"Woody is the hardest and the easiest person to work with," Gallo says. "I'd rather work with him than anyone else. [Among other directors he has worked with are Francis Ford Coppola on *The Godfather* and Arthur Hiller on *The Hospital*.] He lets other people do things. Just

100

don't lie or bullshit him—or be very convincing if you do. Otherwise he'll just keep saying he doesn't understand. You have to read into Woody's mind, and that's hard to do. But after you work with him for a few pictures, you get an idea. Woody's demands are not out of the ordinary on the set, though. I've worked on crews with more experience than the director, but the director still tries to show he knows how to do everything with a lot of fakery and pretense. At least Woody says if he doesn't understand."

There is less and less that Woody doesn't understand now, although, as Gallo says, if he doesn't like what someone is saying to him, or thinks the person is dissembling, he will just stand there and say, "uh huh," and nod his head. Then he'll say "no" or "maybe if you tried it this way instead. . . ." He will listen to suggestions politely and never becomes overtly angered. But until he is sure that another way is better than what he has in mind, he will do things his way, no matter how long it takes. The other side of that tenacity is that everyone who has worked with him agrees that he is almost always right. Having directed five films and with a greater sense of confidence now, he knows exactly what he wants and how to go about it, even though it almost always takes more time than it used to take.

"Originally we could point Woody in the direction to shoot," Gallo says. "Now there's no holding him back. And he's right about ninety-nine percent of the time." (Woody disagrees: "Right from the start I gave them a hard time —but I didn't know much.")

Being right does not necessarily make putting a film together any easier, however. In *Sex* and *Sleeper* a major concern was the necessarily elaborate and ingenious sets.

A problem of Woody's is that while he knows what is right when he sees it, he cannot always specifically say in advance what it is he is looking for, which means that the set designer must have a lot of patience and resilience. Time and again on the two films, Woody would decide that a set that had looked good on paper was not quite right when built. So shooting would come to a halt for an afternoon or a day or more, while the set was rebuilt.

Dale Hennesy (who won an Academy Award for his sets for *Fantastic Voyage*) is a chunky man with blue eyes that show a lot of laughter and reflect a lot of the tension he has to work under. Not only did Hennesy have to try to make concrete what Woody conceptualized, he also had to do it on an ever-shrinking budget. His available cash for *Sleeper* started at $267,000; it ended up at $130,000.

"I love him," Hennesy said one day, looking very haggard after he and Woody had talked about a set Woody wanted modified, "but he's going to kill me. The thing is, Woody has a marvelous visual eye. Maybe it's from watching all those films. He wants everything real but slightly funny. The police van, for instance, is realistic looking, but it also looks a little like an alligator. The biggest problem is trying to outguess Woody. Sketches don't mean anything to Woody. He has to see it with his eyes."

Working under the handicap of not really knowing if a set will work until it is built, especially when the set is of a type that has never been done before—as many of the sets in *Sex* and *Sleeper* were—means that shooting schedules and budgets are under constant revision, and the cost of the film expands to meet the revisions.

102

Some weeks into the shooting of *Sleeper,* Woody stood in a small meadow in the Rockies and threw stones at a tree thirty yards away to pass the time. He was waiting several hours for the sun to go down so the light would be the way he wanted it for shooting, and it was an act that showed how his approach to films has changed.

"When I was shooting *Take the Money,* if I had been a day behind schedule, not to mention three weeks like we are right here, I would have been so worried," he said without concern. "Now it doesn't make much difference. I'm aware that I'm using up a lot of time and money, and I may shoot some things that aren't just as I want them because I feel guilty about just hanging around, and then they won't be any good and we'll have to reshoot. But I'm one hundred percent different in my approach to films now. I know what I'm doing. If I were making a serious film, if I weren't hampered by the problems of comedy, I think I could make a film that cinematically looks like it was made by a really terrific filmmaker. I'm hampered by the fact that what makes a film look beautiful is an obstacle to comedy. When you see *Last Tango in Paris,* which is superb filmmaking, and you try to make a comedy like that, you'd drop dead with it. It would make a comedy oppressive and slow and somber. When I made *Take the Money* I didn't know the first thing. Now I know more frequently what type of day to shoot on, what time of day, what lenses, when to use the dolly. I know much more about that stuff. It's just two different worlds. The trouble is, I'm sometimes forced to make shots that are more simple and less imaginative because I don't want the imagination of the shot to intrude on the laugh. I subordi-

103

nate everything to the laugh. Simplicity is paramount in comedy, and simplicity is not always the best kind of shot.

"I didn't know when I got into this how long it would take, though. I don't feel any sense of accomplishment, having pissed away my fees. I didn't know that it took Chaplin two years to do *City Lights,* or how hard it would be for me to shoot this. And a lot of stuff I see now that looks very good—I know it isn't going to work."

He picked up another stone and threw it. The sun was still a good three hours from where he wanted it.

6.
"I want to make it funny and pretty and the two are opposite."

On April 30, 1973, at 7:30 A.M. on a cold and rainy Monday in a Denver suburb, forty-five carpenters, electricians, teamsters, costumers, prop men, camera operators, sound men, actors, a second assistant director, a hairdresser, a make-up man, a cinematographer, a still photographer, a production designer, a unit publicist, a first assistant director, a script girl, a painter, a special-effects man, a transportation captain, a director, and two caterers in three cars, four trucks, two trailers, and a bus pulled up in the thick mud in front of a strange, futuristic-looking house. Shooting on *Sleeper*, Woody Allen's most expensive and ambitious film so far, scheduled to last fifty days, with locations in and near Denver, Los Angeles, and Monterey, was about to begin. The budget was $2 million.

The actual shooting time turned out to be 101 days, and the final cost was $3,100,000. The first $350,000 in over-age used up Woody's fees for co-writing the script and acting in and directing the movie (although his and Rollins and Joffe's share of the profits—and by the end of 1974 they amounted to about $2 million—was undiminished). It was an expensive (by Woody's standards, not Hollywood's), arduous, trying, demanding, boring film to make, and the process was not much fun for anyone.

The crew had flown to Denver from Los Angeles the day before shooting started. Even though they had stayed up drinking and playing poker long into the night—as they would almost always do—at 6:30 A.M. they were in the dining room for breakfast, sitting—as they would almost always sit—with their peers: sound men with sound men, actors with actors, production people with production people. At one table Jack Grossberg and Fred Gallo were finishing their coffee with Charles Joffe. They talked about filming *Take the Money and Run* and *Bananas* and how Woody always wants to reshoot. They laughed when Grossberg told them that the day before the script girl had come in to tell him her predictions for the running times of the rough and final cuts of the movie, which anyone who has worked with Woody already knows. "Before she could speak, I told her, 'Two hours and a half rough cut; eighty-seven minutes final.' She couldn't believe I knew, but it's the same every time. Then when he starts editing he finds he's dissatisfied with parts and there are the couple of obligatory shooting days in New York that are finally thrown away." In fact, the rough cut *was* two hours and a half. The final cut, with titles and credits, was eighty-eight minutes. The "couple of obligatory shooting days" were done in California to change the ending, and they were kept this time. Woody has said

106

with thoughtful facetiousness that "eighty-nine minutes may be the perfect length for something funny."

At 7:00 A.M. people were milling about in the regulation formica hotel lobby, which looked out onto a one-half square block parking lot and the back of a brick building, waiting for transportation to the set—on this day the strange, futuristic-looking house fifteen miles out of town. Built on what was once grazing land, when it was alone it must have been an impressive sight. Now tract houses have sprung up all around it and it sits like Mae West in a suburban beauty parlor. While most of the crew traveled by bus, David Walsh, Fred Gallo, Woody, the actors, and the key production people traveled by car. Woody stood alone in his khaki rainhat, green army jacket, faded blue baggy-legged jeans, and saddle shoes, waiting for the car and holding his clarinet case. "I keep my one-liners in here," he said, pointing to the case.

Sensing a golden opportunity, a couple of Bunnies from the hotel's Playboy Club strolled through the lobby, attempting to look casual. They were dressed in mufti and their elaborate makeup could not hide the fact that they were obviously short on sleep. They hoped to be discovered. They weren't.

When the caravan arrived at the house, Woody, the camera and sound crews, and the appropriate prop men went inside, making the interior so cramped that everyone realized rather belatedly it would have been easier to build a set in Los Angeles.

Since the first shot was relatively easy, everyone expected shooting to begin right away. But while everything else followed a natural course—the rain picked up; the air grew colder; the mud thickened—shooting did not begin. People outside, who were useful only between shots, tried to stay out of the rain or sloshed and slipped over to where the caterer had set out a large urn of coffee and several dozen doughnuts.

Not satisfied with the set, Woody came outside after an hour and went to wait in his dressing room until the set was ready for shooting. The room, one of three atop a semitrailer that carried equipment beneath, was large enough for perhaps four people to stand in, had a plastic-covered seat for two against the wall, a mirror with lights around it with a chair in front, and an unpleasant-looking mustard-colored rug. (The available space was cut in half a week later when Woody had a Movieola put in so he could watch dailies on the set.) Adjoining the room was a smaller room with a toilet and sink. After a few minutes he began practicing long tones on his clarinet.

The problem with the set was that the black wasn't black enough, the white not white enough. Woody had decided weeks earlier that with one exception (the police uniforms, which were red) all the costumes were to be black, white, or gray, and that the sets were to be as black and white as possible. The idea was to give the film a touch of the pre-Technicolor comedies. The carpet, which he had told the crew the night before to change to black, looked almost right, but the walls didn't. So in went the painter.

At 10:00 A.M. someone went to a nearby house and negotiated with the owner for the use of his garage for the caterer to serve lunch to the crew in for as many days as the weather stayed bad.

At 12:30 the crew broke for an hour's lunch: steak, baked potatoes, several kinds of salads (bean, tossed, raw vegetables, cottage cheese) and desserts (German chocolate cake, cherry pie, fresh fruit, ice cream bars), milk (whole, skimmed, chocolate, and buttermilk), tea, and coffee.

At 4:45 Woody went into the house and they made the first shot of the day. "I've worked on TV shows that are finished by this time," announced the second assistant director, who was working on his first feature film. One of the crew laughed. "You've never worked with Woody before," he said, and he walked over to the prop truck to get out of the rain and wait until he was needed. ("I am not slow," says Woody.)

At 7:30 P.M., twelve hours after the film's official beginning, a halt was called until morning. The picture was now one day behind schedule. "Every picture starts out as a disaster," Fred Gallo said at midnight between drinks.

The second day it snowed, which in a way made walking easier, because the mud, which had gotten so thick the day before that the area around the house looked like a boom-town street in the rainy season, now was frozen in peaks and valleys where feet had tromped through it.

Things were a little better on the set, too: A brief shot was made before lunch—chicken Kiev, etc. (Figuring in all the costs and allowing for a profit, which the caterer certainly did and which included driving his equivalent of a chuck wagon with a trailer full of folding chairs and tables over the Rockies from Los Angeles, the cost per meal was $7.50—or $350 a day.)

After lunch everything was made ready for a bedroom scene between Woody and actress Chris Forbes. For some reason the scene, which looked very funny by itself, never got a laugh when it was put in the movie and screened during the editing process. Even though Woody liked the sequence a lot, it was cut. It was a parody of most bedroom scenes: the male making sure he looked just right, assuming as debonair an aura as possible; the female, soft and silky in a white satin gown, spread langorously on the bed.

Woody rehearsed the scene a couple of times. Looking in a mirror, he put on an aviator's cap, affixed a mustache, put around his neck a white silk scarf that was to be blown by an off-camera fan. Then Woody turned to the crew. "Here's what I'm going to do. I'm going to fix myself up, scent the room twice. Then the fan blows the scarf and she's sitting on the bed eating yoghurt, or strawberries and cream, or whatever it is they eat. Then I go over and start working on her a bit, biting her, and the fan blows harder and harder . . . we do have the fan, don't we?" He looked up and the property man said he had a fan but from what Woody described it wasn't going to blow nearly hard enough. "I want something like a tornado," Woody said. The prop man ran off to rent two huge fans. Woody told the rest of the crew that "We need a gallon of Jell-O, or a huge sundae with a couple of gallons of ice cream. She should be in bed eating with a huge spoon." He turned to Chris. "Is there anything you don't eat?" There wasn't. Someone checked with the caterer and found he had four gallons of cottage cheese and some orange slices. The clear plastic bowl that had held enough salad for fifty people at lunch was filled up and brought in. It looked appropriate enough. Woody was still thinking. "You know, it would be funny to me if I could open up a little cube when I get over to her and have a little man come out and run all over her body."

The fans arrived and did fine on a trial run. But Woody

110

was thinking some more. "You're in for a big surprise, Chris," he said with a slight smile. Then to no one in particular: "It would be funny if I had a snorkel and wet suit and fins instead of the aviator's costume." The crew laughed. Woody smiled. "You think I'm kidding, but I'm not." The wardrobe man and the policeman assigned to the film for traffic and crowd assistance got into the police car and roared off toward Denver with the lights flashing and the siren blaring to get the equipment.

"This is what I'm notorious for," Woody said as the crew moved off to sit and wait. "That's why it's not fun for my crew. But then, only so much can be done in advance. Things occur to me on the set and it seems a shame not to do them if we can."

After the wet suit arrived and Woody put it on, he flopped around in the fins, then stopped for a second and peered out through the mask. "If people don't laugh at this, I'm going to give up."

Several days later than expected, shooting stopped at the house, although there were still a couple of scenes left to do. The locations for the next day, and the following several days, were scattered around in the Rockies above Denver, about a forty-five-minute drive away. The bus was to leave at 7:00 A.M. as it did six days a week. On the way down to breakfast one of the crew got in the elevator Woody was riding in.

"I'm sure tired of this town," Woody said. "I wouldn't mind shooting seven days a week and getting out of here faster."

"You know, he'd do it, too," the man said unhappily on the crew bus later. "We were scheduled to be here ten days. It'll be a month." It nearly was.

111

Once up in the mountains, Woody stood by while the equipment was set up for a shot of him and Diane Keaton trekking through the woods. It was a sunny morning. It was also twenty degrees. Most of the ground still had snow on it. Woody was bundled in a thick down parka. He was not happy.

"I hate it here. If I were in L.A. I would be hating it, being unable to wait to get to New York, where nothing is probably happening anyway."

He went off with David Walsh, the cinematographer, to set up the camera. The shot looked almost good. They tried a 250mm lens, then a 1000mm lens. Woody walked over the area muttering to himself. They tried another lens.

"The trouble is, I want to make it funny *and* pretty, and the two are opposite," he complained. "It's a real pain in the ass." They tried another angle: "Too arty." And another. Woody looked through the camera, followed by Walsh, then Roger Sherman, the cameraman.

"Does this shot bother you the way it bothers me?" Woody asked Walsh. "No? Then argue with me. I think it needs more of a sense of trees. There aren't enough in the frame."

Walsh did not argue for the shot. Instead, he and Woody and Fred Gallo took off in a station wagon to look at some other places. A couple of hours later they were ready with another spot which looked much better.

But of course it is not just how good a film looks that counts. "There is a great skill in blending together good performances and a good story. Enormous finesse," Woody says. "But there's no mystery to it from a technical point of view. Millions of guys who had gone to movies all

112

their lives could make a movie. Where they fall short, like many of these TV commercial directors who make movies, is that they don't have a dramatic sense or a sense of comedy. Technically, they're wonderful. They could direct circles around me from a technical point of view. They get everything going beautifully: their photography is great and their moves are beautiful. But what they don't have is dramatic sense or a sense of comedy. That's why Buñuel's films can look terrible and still be masterpieces, because overwhelmingly what's important is the content. Every piece of junk that comes out looks good, because what they'll do is go out and hire a first-rate cameraman and a first-rate editor, and they all know what to do. There's nothing to getting good people."

Which is not to deny the importance of first-rate people doing what they know how to do and complementing a good director. Woody certainly hires the best crew money, his reputation, and a former crew's loyalty can get in an attempt to make the best, funniest, fastest-paced film he can.

"Pacing is always a problem," Woody said one day while waiting for a crane to be brought in and set up for a shot in a meadow at the end of a long, winding dirt road in the Rockies. "There are very few comedies in the world, and even the greatest have *langeur* in them. There's no way out. There are moments that you tolerate. Once in a while you hit on something like *Duck Soup* that has practically no dead spot in it. If you were asked to name the best comedies ever made, and you named *The Gold Rush* and *The General* and a half dozen others, *Duck Soup* is the only one that really doesn't have a dull spot.

113

"*Sleeper* is like three-dimensional chess. On one level you have the story that you want the people to believe enough but not so much that it's a problem; and you want an abundance of verbal jokes; and an abundance of visual jokes. It's tough. Bob Hope's movies are almost all verbal jokes. Keaton just had to worry about his visual jokes. Chaplin is visual jokes. I have tripped myself up many times on all these things. I've made story mistakes, visual mistakes, and dialogue mistakes.

"In the end, this kind of film is a director's medium and a comedian's medium. When Mickey Rose and Marshall Brickman write a script with me, they are writing for a performer. I'm like the head writer. I want them to write material for me. Ideally, I like to do the basic writing myself, then call in someone like Mickey when I'm stuck and need a joke, then bang, there it is. But you can't do that because then they're not into the story with you. If they don't know the roots of it, they can't come up with something.

"Monologue material is different from film scripts in that you have to do it yourself, because what happens is you go up on stage and find you write a portion of your monologue there—you start editing fast. You go up with ten jokes and you start telling them and when you're on joke four you know joke five isn't going to get a laugh because suddenly the reality of life is rushing up there very swiftly and you're not in a closed room with a guy or alone titillating yourself. You're out there and you can feel it. Something tells you that if you tell the next joke they're not going to laugh, so you cut through five and six and go to seven. It's totally an instinctive thing. You just know if you grimace a little more they'll keep on laughing, and if

114

you're a comedian you know if you grimace another quarter inch it'll be overdone.

"There's something in me that's survival. Your body dictates what to do. When I was in Sicily promoting *Bananas* and the whole audience spoke Italian and I went onstage, I just knew that I could get laughs from them. That's why it's so hard to write in a room, because when I'm out here, hanging on a ladder doing something, the instinct is different. That doesn't mean I'm always going to make it funny, but what I'm going to do is different than when I conceived it. If I conceive that I'm going to be hanging on a ladder and I kick it away, it doesn't mean anything. When I'm up there my body will tell me to do something else and I'll do it and it'll either work or it will not, but that's the thing to do. If you're talking about a live audience, I'm right almost all of the time. But that has nothing to do with films and it makes you crazy. Something happens in the filming that gives another dimension, good or bad. I know that when I fell yesterday that I was doing the proper thing that these people around here would think was funny. I know that if there were a thousand people in the audience and I was in the middle of a play and I fell like that that I would get a big laugh. But I can't guarantee that it would look like that on film. That's what makes you crazy. You know what to do and yet when you film it there is something that happens that casts a different perspective on it and sometimes it doesn't work when you see it. We're all at the mercy of the dailies. I'll watch the dailies and I'll think none of those walks looks funny and I'll reshoot them and when I go to edit the film and I cut those walks in, the two worst ones in dailies will get the biggest laughs. There are so many

115

factors you're bucking. That's why film comedies are so hard."

While the crane was being set up, the crew sat around playing poker or lying in the sun or drinking coffee. Woody, who almost always keeps by himself between shots, or is with Diane Keaton when she is on the set, stood off on the dirt road instead of on the grass where everyone else was. Jack Grossberg had come to the meadow a little earlier and tried to calmly tell everyone that there were ticks (which carry Rocky Mountain spotted fever) around and that he had rubber bands for trouser cuffs to help fend them off. Woody is not one to take such news lightly: his cuffs were tightly banded and he was carefully staying off the grass. As he was watching the crane come in, there was a rumble of thunder. "It's either ticks or get struck by lightning," he said in disgust. "I'd rather get struck by lightning. Come to think of it, it would break up the monotony.

"If I wanted to have a weekend of pure pleasure," which he clearly did, "it would be to have a half-dozen Bob Hope films and watch them, films like *Monsieur Beaucaire* and *My Favorite Brunette*. It's not for nothing that he's such a greatly accepted comedian. He is a great, great talent, a guy who has been able to combine a thin story with great jokes. No one ever sees this, but there is this similarity I see in him, Mort Sahl, and finally, in a derivative manner, myself. I see this tremendous similarity between Bob Hope and Mort Sahl. Think of it this way: They are two stand-up monologists who talk as themselves; they have these slick individual personalities; they're bright and sharp; they both have political jokes, although Sahl's are much deeper; they have this great

116

monologue style, great phrasing. When people ask me who I was influenced by, it was these two more than anyone else. I was really doing them to a great degree once. Bob Hope I still do. I lean on him a certain amount and used to much more. [In *Sleeper* one scene shows Hope's influence quite clearly. Woody and Diane Keaton, disguised as doctors, are about to operate on all that is left of The Leader—his nose. As they walk down the hospital corridor, Woody nervously bites Diane's fingernails while he tells her to keep calm; as they enter the operating room, Woody taps the guard on his chest a couple of times with great bravado and brashly announces, "We're here to see the nose. I understand it's running."] Mickey and I used to watch his movies over and over when we were kids, and to me it's a great joy. He's stunning sometimes.

"Hope was always a superschnook. He looks less like a schnook than I do. I look more schnooky, more intellectual. But both of us have the exact same wellspring of humor. There are certain moments when I think he's the best thing I have ever seen. It's everything I can do at certain times not to actually do him. It's hard to tell when I do, because I'm so unlike him physically and in tone of voice, but once you know I do it, it's absolutely unmistakeable. You've got to go by his older movies. He had those sort of snotty one-liners that I always liked. Sahl had them later in a different way."

The crane was finally ready and Woody's stunt double was fitted with a harness under his costume to which two thin steel wires from the crane could be attached so he would appear airborne while wearing a flying pack. His hair, which was naturally brown, had been tinted red by the makeup man and a bald patch had been put in the back to match Woody's, so that from a slight distance (what is called a "medium shot") there would be no discernible difference between them. Later Woody put on the harness and the flying pack and some close-up shots were made of him under less strenuous conditions.

Things in the movies are seldom what they seem. Fancy living rooms are often three-sided plywood walls with furniture placed around. Immediately out of scope in every shot are fifty or so crew members, yards and yards of electrical cables, a boom man holding a microphone, a sound man monitoring a five-thousand-dollar tape recorder to make sure it all gets on at the right levels, and a cameraman making sure none of them gets in the shot. For shots that require any sort of gimmick, there is a special-effects man who knows exactly how to make appearance seem reality—at least on the screen. Fortunately, some things do not pick up well on film, and directors count on the audience to be absorbed enough with the action and the plot that they do not notice a thin steel wire generally obscured by the sky but sometimes clearly visible.

Several shots in *Sleeper* required wires, and they often had to be made over and over again until the wires were inconspicuous enough. ("This is a movie about wires," Woody said during a final screening during editing.) The most difficult stunt shot to shoot was a scene where Woody is in the water in an inflatable rubber suit that has billowed out to the size of a 400-pound man. He and Diane Keaton, who is on his back, are trying to escape from the police. The suit is punctured by a shot from a policeman's gun, and the two of them shoot off across the lake like a balloon that has just had the air released from it.

118

It was supposed to be a fairly simple procedure: Woody's double, with Diane's double on his back, would be on a small raft located under his chest. A thick line attached to the raft would run 100 yards underwater, make a turn through a pulley for twenty-five yards, and be fastened to the tail of a pickup truck. The truck would then accelerate, pulling the raft and people.

But it wasn't that easy. A rope traveling underwater pulling 250 pounds of people and raft is actually dragging a high multiple of that weight, and it is enough to snap even a good rope, which it did. Often. The day the shot was supposed to be made went by, as did four others, before it was successfully made.

On the third day it looked for a while as though it would all work. Two cameras were set up, one head-on and one which would follow at an angle until the bodies passed directly in front of it, then shoot from the rear. Woody and David Walsh were at the camera on the angle, which had an umbrella over it to keep off some of the 115-degree sun. Roger Sherman, the cameraman who normally operated the main camera, was at the second camera up on a road just above the lake for the head-on shot. He had no umbrella. An hour after he had gone up to take his spot, the shot had not been made. More adjustments.

"Sunburned to Big Umbrella," Sherman called over the walkie-talkie. "I've found a little waterfall. Call me when you're ready."

Soon everything was ready. Woody, whose patience had worn thin, put on a face of strained anticipation. "Action!" Fred Gallo yelled, and off went the raft with the doubles. This time the rope did not break. It simply

119

popped up out of the water and was big and black and very visible all through the shot.

"How was that for you, Roger?" Walsh asked over the walkie-talkie, hoping that Sherman's camera had perhaps not picked up the rope.

"A nothingburger," Sherman answered.

The whole fourth day was a nothingburger. Approximately $80,000 had now been spent keeping forty-five people in the hot sun all day, bussing them an hour each way to and from their beds, and giving several of the crew a chance for a lunch-time poker game ($2 to $4 limit). There was a lot of unusable film footage and one good shot of Woody and Diane in the water, which had been an easier shot to make: Instead of being pulled directly by the truck, the rope was attached to a boat a few feet ahead so the dialogue could be picked up and a close-up shot made from the rear of the boat. They did not need as much speed as for the long shot either. (In the long shots, which were without dialogue, the camera speed was eighteen frames per second rather than the normal twenty-four, thus quickening the action by twenty-five percent.)

By the end of the fifth day the shot had been made enough times with the rope at least sometimes obscured so that with some artful cutting it would not be noticeable. All that remained to be done was a rear shot of two dummys in Woody's and Diane's costumes being pulled on the raft. It worked the first time. Prospects improved for finishing the film. With relief everyone went back to the studio in Los Angeles.

More problems arose, however, and the picture fell farther behind schedule. One major cause of delay was the very lifelike robots. The robots moved with a pro-

120

nounced mechanical gait but could perform any sort of household duty upon command, and Woody spent a great deal of time picking the actors to play them. Various masks and makeups were tried, and an expressionless silver mask with a speaker where the mouth should be was finally decided on. But Woody, who at one point in the film is disguised as a robot, was indistinguishable from the others when he wore a mask. A plaster cast was made of his face for a different sort of mask, but that didn't work either. Finally he was made up in clown white, had a speaker put in his mouth, and left his glasses on.

"We should have had six months to perfect the cars and robots," Fred Gallo said one day while shooting was delayed because of the robots' costumes. "We had time for enough test shooting to know we didn't want what we saw, but not enough to figure out what we did want. Woody just doesn't know what he wants until he sees it.

"On a show like this, if you get stuck, you can't do something else. You can't just go out on a street and shoot a walk-through, because everything requires special sets. And those cars are awful. [There were several tear-shaped, bubble-topped cars powered by a small motor and steered with two levers instead of a wheel. Seen from the outside, which is the only way they were really seen, they looked cute and terrific and as if they rode on air, but they were absolutely impractical.] Actors have enough trouble getting into a car, let alone driving one; especially one without a steering wheel. Only people who were in the army or are bulldozer operators know how to handle lateral-drive cars. You don't put Woody or an actor in one of these and say, 'Act natural.' Plus, you can't shoot inside them. The first thing you should do is build a breakaway

121

car. Regular cars have attachments that fit so you can shoot into them, but not these."

"I was thinking about *Sleeper* today in terms of how I hate machines in real life," Woody said that night. "I have no patience with them. I break them. That's an honest thing with me. People close to me will confirm how many toasters I've broken. And I noticed in *Sleeper* one of the recurrent themes is that advanced technology doesn't work; a guy shoots a future gun and it blows up; I go into a futuristic kitchen and that malfunctions [instant pudding turns into a giant, moving blob that has to be beaten into submission with a broom]. Right through the writing and filming, without thinking for a second, I have just thought of funny jokes as I went along. Now someone will see that and say, 'He doesn't get along with machines,' and will think that I set out to do it. And all I had thought was that it would be funny if the gun the police were shooting at the guy running off would blow up. Then it would blow up when they tried it again. Then the third time the truck that it's attached to would blow up. You would think that I'm doing that on purpose, that I'm trying to create a character that doesn't get along with machines. But it's always involuntary. I don't consciously try to put in those things."

The robots were finally the way Woody liked them, but then there were problems with other sets. There was a lot of complicated gadgetry used in *Sleeper* and it took much longer to perfect than Woody had expected. One thing that did work well, though, was a motorized wheelchair Woody was put into after the doctors in the underground defrosted him. It was one of several props available to Woody—he likes to have as wide an assortment as possible

to choose from so that when he sees the set with everything in place he can decide what will be the funniest
thing for him to do. In this case, what seemed funniest to
him was his being semiconscious in a wheelchair and accidentally setting it in motion while the doctors nervously
try to convince the security guards who have come into
the room that nothing is wrong. He drives the chair into
the group of doctors and guards, runs over feet, and spins
in circles while the doctors try not to notice and the
guards get more suspicious. (One of the funniest gags that
occurred to Woody on a set happened during the filming
of *Bananas.* For a palace dinner scene a string quartet
was supposed to be playing, but the instruments had not
arrived by the time everything was ready for shooting. So
Woody had the quartet—"We borrowed them from an
old-age home," Gallo says—play in mime.)

As the shooting of *Sleeper* dragged on and on, Woody
began to show signs of being physically and mentally
tired. Normally he keeps an even pace and appearance.
He can spend the day on the set, be available to look at
designs for new ones, talk with Jack Grossberg about future shooting days and tell him not to worry about the
money, practice his clarinet, and work on his French. (He
chose French because he is popular in France, likes Paris
more than anywhere save New York, and talks occasionally about living there for a while—and did, in fact, for six
months while making *Love and Death.* So often between
shots he and Elizabeth Claman would sit around and talk
—she in good French and he in steadily improving
French. The conversations were general and covered
whatever happened to be on their minds. One day while
sitting on a waterbed in the house where shooting was

going on, Woody asked, *"L'avez-vous fait dans un lit comme ça?"*)

But by the end of July the pressures of the film occasionally broke through Woody's calm, even detached exterior. One night, after a long day at the studio and with the prospect of having to go to the Los Angeles airport at midnight to make yet another shot still ahead, he went back to his suite at the Beverly Wilshire Hotel for a few hours of rest.

Originally Woody had lived in a rented Beverly Hills mansion. But the birds started chirping at one or two in the morning and they disturbed him so much that, after trying several things, including shooting an airgun at them and mimicking a cat and a hawk to try to scare them off, he finally just moved out of the mansion and into a $100-a-day hotel suite. Many people, including Grossberg, thought that was a little strange, since the production company was still paying rent on the house, but it was not at all out of character.

"Now, some think me crazy about moving out of my house here and into the hotel. But those birds were *loud*. Here there are no ants in the room and no mosquitoes, and if it's very hot in the room I cool it and if it's very cool I turn up the heat. In my house in New York if I get very hungry at two o'clock in the morning, I can call someone up and go to Chinatown. It's a different kind of life. I like cities. I always have, always have responded to them: London, Paris, New York—less to L.A. because it is less of a city.

"Cities are more civilized, more controlled. They interest me more. As a kid I always thought of myself in Manhattan and always had fantasies of being a bookmaker or something like that who lived and hung out in the city. And my delights to this day are going to Madison Square Garden and to the fights and the movies; it's always the city."

Why he likes them so much seemed clearer then than perhaps any other time he ever talked about his love for cities. He is a man who pulls his inspiration out of himself and is extraordinarily well disciplined and controlled; and in a city it is more possible than anywhere else to control one's environment with the least effort, thus saving energy for work. But even with all that control available, he was tired now as he sat on the sofa in his suite and talked about making movies.

By the middle of July it had become clear that the film would be going for another month to six weeks and that Woody was going to have to begin editing it before shooting was completed. While some directors edit as they go along and have a rough cut ready at the end of filming, Woody had always held off doing any editing at all until he could devote himself to that alone. Certainly with the chores of rewriting scenes, acting, and directing, he had little time for anything else anyway, least of all something like editing, which requires considerable time and attention. But he was up against a deadline. *Sleeper* was to be United Artists' Christmas film and was already scheduled to open in New York the week before Christmas, and there was no way around that.

At first Woody resisted Grossberg's pushing him to start editing in Los Angeles but he finally realized that something had to be done. So he asked Ralph Rosenblum, who had edited *Take the Money and Run* and *Bananas,* to come out to Los Angeles and talk; Rosenblum, too, was pushing to get him started in Los Angeles. Woody's original plan was for Rosenblum and himself to do all the editing in Rosenblum's studio in New York.

Rosenblum was introduced to Woody by Grossberg after *Take the Money and Run* was finished and they were unhappy with the film as it was cut. Rosenblum, who has edited films as diverse as *Long Day's Journey into Night* and *The Producers*, had a big effect on Woody's confidence as they re-edited the film. The two of them work quickly and well together and show an enormous trust and respect for the other's opinions and talents.

"When [the late] Stanley Prager agreed to come in and direct *Don't Drink the Water* when we were having trouble getting it ready for Broadway, it was more that he had confidence and gave it to us than anything else. The same was true when Ralph edited *Take the Money*," Woody said just before Rosenblum came to Los Angeles. "I had been too harsh on myself and lopped out gobs and gobs of material. His big thing was to say, 'Put it back.'"

Rosenblum and Grossberg worked together on *The Producers*. They have known each other for years and understand each other easily. They talked on the phone from time to time during the filming of *Sleeper*, and once Ralph asked Jack how Woody was doing with the film.

"The butterfly has come out—and he has red hair," Grossberg said.

Rosenblum laughed and knew without being told more that the film he was going to edit would look a lot different than any other he had done with Woody.

Rosenblum arrived from New York one afternoon as Woody was shooting a scene inside a van filled with ro-

126

bots. Woody came out of the van—actually a plywood box on the sound stage—and walked over to him.

"Hi, Ralph," he said. "Got any New York lint on you?"

They exchanged a couple of pleasantries and then moved off a bit from the crew.

"Now, on this film I want it to be really fast-paced, to go uphill all the time," Woody, looking very serious, told him. "And I want it to have a strong plot, a strong story line. . . ."

"Woody, it's me, Ralph," he said, laughing. "We've talked about this hundreds of times."

7.
Like digging
a grave at a cemetery—over
and over again.

"Digging a grave at a cemetery would be funnier to watch than two guys cutting a comedy," Ralph Rosenblum said one day as he and Woody edited *Sleeper*. Film editing is by itself a serious business, but editing a comedy is so serious that it borders on the grim. Woody and Ralph spent their days looking at pieces of film over and over again, trying to find the ones that played the best in relation to the others. As with any film, they cut, spliced, respliced, and depended on a good deal of luck. As is generally the case with Woody's films, whole sequences of the script were dropped and much of the story line disappeared in an attempt to keep the film moving quickly.

Woody worked on one sequence and Ralph worked on the following one. After each was finished, he showed the other what he had done. Then they collaborated on any changes that were made.

128

The two were working with a tremendous amount of exposed film—about 200,000 feet on 240 reels, or thirty-five hours. That had to be reduced to ninety minutes. Most films use perhaps 150,000 feet tops—and run 110 minutes.

By late September they had a rough cut of two hours and twenty minutes. They went to a screening room and immediately after seeing it took out another twenty minutes. Then came the process of cutting, screening it for a few people to get their reactions, then reworking and cutting parts, then screening, and so on, until they had the best ninety minutes.

"The most important thing for me to get from Woody is what he considers his best reading of a joke or his best performance," Rosenblum said during editing. "I can't think of one thing that he reshot that he doesn't appear in."

Yet in many cases the first shot is the best, at least as long as the scene remains unchanged. Sometimes, as in the case of the ending for *Sleeper*, much of the scene is rewritten, then shot again, and it plays much better than the original.

"But when it comes to physical stuff, I always feel that the first take will be the best, like lifting weights—the first snatch is the one that's going to be strongest," Woody said one day after reshooting a scene. "One of the strongest evidences of that to me is that when I was fighting at the future farm [Woody gets in a fight with the caretaker and they repeatedly slip and fall on an eight-foot banana peel] the first couple of takes went really well. And when I saw them I said, 'Hey, I didn't think I could do it that well. I'm going to go back and really perfect it.' But none of the

129

reshoots was good, even though I had the benefit of seeing the early stuff and knowing it looked funny. I never improved on any of those things."

Woody has tried various approaches to showing rough cuts of his films. For the earlier ones, he had a mixed group of friends, strangers, soldiers from the U.S.O., and college students who were invited via messages on bulletin boards. Now he has become less random in picking the audiences of the unfinished film. In one way or another, they are directly or remotely connected to it. Some, friends of Ralph Rosenblum's or of the assistant editor's, invite friends in turn; Woody asks people he knows; Jack Rollins and Charles Joffe do the same.

No system of previews is very satisfactory to Woody, however. "None of it's good," he said after *Sleeper* had been screened several times. "There's no real way to do it and get an objective reaction. The only thing I can do is watch myself and see how the audiences react after three or five times. I can't go by one of those audiences. Robert Evans [the head of production at Paramount Pictures] did the best on *Sam*. He made a temporary mix, which was expensive, and then put the film in a regular theater, so there was at least a shot at it."

Woody and Ralph noted where the audiences consistently failed to respond. Then, no matter how much they liked the scene or joke individually, out it went. One scene that was cut may have been visually the best in the film. The scene, which follows, was shot on a salt flat on the Mojave Desert. The chess board mentioned in it was in the middle of the flat, first seen from afar through shimmering heat waves. The scene begins with two doctors going to a dream visualizer to see what the newly defrosted Miles Monroe is dreaming about. This is how it appeared in the script:

They are standing over Miles who is in a restive sleep, his head hooked into a device that produces his dream on a large wall screen. He tosses and turns and moans and finally, after some abstractions, we see forms corresponding to his moaning.

Gradually a dream appears. It is an enormous chess board and Miles is a white pawn.

White is obviously losing, and as he stands erect on his square, he is surrounded by incredibly powerful and hostile black pieces, knights on horseback, bishops hostilely brandishing heavy crucifixes like policemen's billies ready to smash his head in.

On the square next to Miles is another feeble white pawn.

Suddenly the black knight moves, leaping from his position to the square occupied by the pawn next to Miles. The knight falls upon the pawn and destroys him brutally with something like a mace and chain and then runs him through with a long sword until he's dead.

Miles is quaking in his boots, naturally unable to move and at the mercy of the man playing the game, whom we don't see of course because he'd be too enormous in scale.

KNIGHT
(now looking viciously down right next to Miles) You're next. . . .

BLACK BISHOP
(several squares away, tapping a crucifix menacingly) Leave him to me, I'll take care of him.

131

MILES
It's a nice board, isn't it?

MAN'S VOICE
(*playing*) I think my best move is to sacrifice that second pawn.

MILES
I'm fine here. Hey . . . that's me. I'm happy right where I am.

MAN'S VOICE
If I move my pawn the knight'll take him but I'll get his rook. I'll sacrifice a stupid pawn and win a rook.

MILES
No. . . .

Suddenly he is moved forward into the midst of a knight, bishop, and queen. He is face to face with a menacing black pawn.

Ad lib fear business and chatter. . . .

MILES
(*continuing*) Hey, fellas . . . it's only a game. We'll all be together later in the box.

KNIGHT
I'm going to cut you in two. . . .

OPPONENT'S VOICE
Look where he moved that pawn. . . . Should I take him with my bishop or knight? . . . Let's see. . . . On the other hand, why does he want me to take it? . . . Maybe I should wait a

move. . . . No, what the hell, I'll take
the pawn. . . .

The knight charges for the pawn. Miles, breaking the laws of chess, starts running in the awkward way a chess piece might. (Miles cops a feel on the queen before running away.) The knight chases Miles off into the distance, then into a corridor. Suddenly Miles runs through a doorway and emerges on the other side in white tie and tails on stage at the opera house.

Miles acknowledges applause, bows and gestures to stage right where the second member of his musical group comes out, a man in a cello suit, giving the appearance of a cello with legs. The cello walks out on stage and squats ready to play himself.

Another man, the next member, enters in white tie and tails, but instead of a head, coming out of his collar is an enormous light bulb. Miles pulls a chain hanging from the man's arm and the bulb goes on.

Miles lifts his violin and bows majestically, but just before he plays the bow suddenly sags limp like a noodle. He is terribly embarrassed by this obviously sexual symbolism and the audience laughs but he cannot make the bow erect enough to play.

In mid-October, when the film was down to about 100 minutes, Woody went to New Orleans for two days to play clarinet with the Preservation Hall Jazz Band and record the sound track for *Sleeper.* It was the one thing about making the film that he had looked forward to.

Woody began playing the clarinet when he was sixteen, and for years he played only at home in accompaniment to George Lewis's records. Lewis, one of the best New Orleans-style clarinetists, died in 1968, but his sound—a big, expressive tone not clean-cut like Benny Goodman's, but rather blue and sweet with a plaintive tinge and a pronounced vibrato at times—can be heard often in Woody's playing. (A three-by-five-inch picture of Lewis is in one of the bookshelves in Woody's living room. The only other photo he has there is a similar-sized one of Diane Keaton.)

New Orleans jazz is a lot of fun to listen to—it has a wonderful 4/4 beat that gets the listeners' feet moving and a melody that all the players stick to rather than improvise on (the case with Kansas City and Chicago style). In New Orleans style, harmony is not as important as the melody and the beat, and so while each player has his own part, and each has solos, they all play together for the benefit of the band. Because there are so few musicians who work at playing it, and because those who do are almost all quite old, New Orleans jazz is a vanishing art form. It developed at the turn of the century in New Orleans, unsurprisingly, out of the traditional marches and hymns that city's bands played at wakes and in parades and jam sessions into soulful, happy music.

Considering that Woody is white, Jewish, from Brooklyn, and almost half the age of the rest of the band, his playing is given high marks by jazz cognoscenti. But he's not as much fun to watch as the other players. When he plays, he just sits, legs crossed, eyes and clarinet pointed at the floor. The others in the band more than make up for Woody's exterior dullness.

"Big Jim" Robinson, eighty-three years old, plays the trombone as though it had been invented for him, getting

134

a wonderful sound by playing almost out of the right side of his mouth alone, with his left cheek flat and his right one out like a balloon. During his breaks he points to his lips as if to say they aren't that good today, and then he laughs.

Chester Zardis, on bass, isn't more than 5 feet 6 inches tall and is seventy-four years old, but he plays a bass like no one has heard before with the strength of a heavyweight. He sits on a stool and, when he solos, his right leg shoots out in time to the music.

Emanuel Sayles, on banjo, and Sing Miller, on piano, flash their teeth when they sing solos: Emanuel has several gold teeth in the back righthand side of his mouth, which he contorts to display them; Sing has only one large lower-front tooth. Percy Humphrey, the trumpet player and leader of the band, has a dour look but magisterial movements. Josiah "Cie" Frazier, on drums, smiles and smiles. All of them are at least sixty years old.

Preservation Hall is unlike any recording studio film scores are produced in. In fact, it is unlike almost any hall music is played in. A room perhaps forty-five feet long and half as wide, it has worn wooden floors, walls partly covered by pegboard (it was once an art gallery) with the rest bare wood or peeled plaster. It looks pretty seedy but the acoustics are great. There are a couple of rows of benches that begin three feet away from the band; the rest of the 200 or so jazz fans who cram in at one time stand up.

Woody came into the hall in a pair of pressed army fatigue trousers, a flannel shirt with a tie, a maroon corduroy jacket, and his khaki raincap, hung up his coat behind the piano, and, without any to-do, sat down beside trumpeter Percy Humphrey. The band has always hung

135

up both their coats and their felt or straw fedoras; Woody left his hat on until Sandra Jaffe, whose husband Allan founded and runs Preservation Hall, came over and took it off for him. "I'll hang it up with the musicians,'" she said. It was the only error made during the two days.

Without saying anything, Percy played a couple of soft notes and on the beat they all started playing "Little Liza Jane." He did the same for each number. Sometimes a measure or two would go by before Woody figured out what the song was, but that was all it ever took.

"He has a wonderful ear," Percy said afterward. "He did what you should do when you sit with another man's band. He played along with what we played. He didn't try to be a celebrity."

At the end of each set the band was introduced to the audience. The applause for Woody was no greater than for the others, but the general reaction was "I *thought* that was Woody Allen, but it seemed so implausible." People bought records of the band and asked for all the musicians' autographs, including Woody's, though of course he does not play on the albums. He would rather have ducked out to catch a few minutes of the World Series. A young man about 5 feet 5 inches tall came up to Woody, who is 5 feet 6 inches. "If I'm shorter than you, I'm committing suicide," he said, then walked off.

Woody looked blankly at him for a second. "Cavett always has a witty riposte for these people," he said after the fellow left. (That day at lunch, a not unattractive woman handed him a note. "If you're who I think you are," the note read, "I've always wanted to fuck you to death." Woody looked up at the woman. "Who do you think I am?" he asked. Sometimes, however, things are different. At lunch in Colorado once a waitress asked him if he was Woody Allen. He just looked at her and sort of shook his head no. "Sorry if I insulted you," the waitress said.)

Between recording sessions, Woody listened to the tapes in the sound truck parked on the sidewalk outside the hall. It looked like a delivery van on the outside but it had floor to wall to ceiling carpeting on the inside, as well as $100,000 worth of consoles, speakers, tape machines, and power banks that had 608 buttons, knobs, and switches, twenty-five dials, four speakers, a TV monitor, and two speaker controls with sixteen dials and knobs.

Woody especially liked the recording of "Savoy Blues" and "Climax Rag." "I'm going to have to teach this to my band," he said when he heard "Lord, Lord, Lord You Been Good to Me." (Woody's band, the New Orleans Funeral and Rag Time Orchestra, plays every Monday night Woody is in New York at Michael's Pub, a restaurant on the East Side.) "My band takes the breaks earlier," he explained when he heard "Joe Avery."

Sometimes he was not pleased. "I sound too white, too bland," he complained once.

"It's like taking a white person and putting him in a Gospel quartet," Phil Ramon, the recording producer, said.

"Why would you want to do that?" Woody asked.

During the afternoon session Allan Jaffe played bass horn on some numbers. Woody had told him that for chase scenes he needed something a little faster-paced than they had been getting, but he knew he couldn't ask the band to play faster. "Asking a band to play faster is worse than asking them to play 'When the Saints Go

Marching In,' " Jaffe said later. So when there was a lull, Jaffe asked trumpeter Humphey, "What would you play if it was 12:27 and you wanted to get to the clubhouse at 12:30?" Percy thought for a second and then they played "Bye and Bye" at a pretty fast pace.

A problem with doing a score this way is that the control is in the hands of the band; the Preservation Hall Jazz Band—which was being paid $12,000 by United Artists—is not a group of studio musicians. On the other hand, they wanted to be as cooperative as possible and Percy kept asking Woody if he was getting what he wanted. Still, it was hard for them to realize all the variety of music he needed since no one in the band attends many movies. One musician went with Jaffe to see *Shaft*. It was the first film he had seen in a theater since sound came in.

Woody had expected that he would not be able to get all the music he wanted from the band, however, and he had already arranged for his band to record a Monday night performance when he went back to New York.

"All along I've expected that I would record some of the music with my band," he said between sessions. "For some scenes I need to choose music to fit where I'm running, for instance, and with my band I can tell them to play faster or slower, or when I need a break, or a tuba solo, or where I can play a couple of riffs. I can't do that in another man's band. It will be interesting to have a contrast with both bands."

At 12:30 A.M. on the second day the last session ended. Seven hours later the band had to fly to Portland, Oregon, for a concert. A couple of hours after that Woody would leave for New York to get back to the last of the editing. Woody was pleased when Albert Burbank, probably the

138

premier New Orleans-style clarinetist now, came over to congratulate him. Then trombonist Jim Robinson came over.

"Did anyone ever tell you you sound like my old friend George Lewis?" he asked Woody. "What's your name again?"

"Woody," he mumbled.

"Willard? You're real good, Willard."

By late November the film was ready to be mixed—to have the voice track, which until then had been on magnetic tape and then syncronized with the action and attached to the 35mm film, transferred onto the film itself, and to have all the other sounds that make up a film— music, doors slamming, footsteps, cars moving, and so forth—added as well. Mixing is done in a special studio that has a screen and a console with controls for as many separate sounds as are necessary. The control knobs are hooked up to as many tapes as there are individual sounds to be mixed together in a scene: voices, wind, footsteps, babies crying—whatever. The mixer plays the appropriate sounds as the film is shown on the screen, and the director and editor decide how loud or soft they should be in relation to one another. When that has been done— usually after a dozen or so play-throughs—they are recorded at the proper levels and transferred to the master print, where they appear as little wavy lines along the side of the film. The lines translate back out as sound when the film is shown. It is a meticulous and boring process.

One day they mixed a scene in which Woody and Diane, in a house that is suddenly surrounded by the police, try to hide. Woody puts Diane in a room whose secret door is a sliding bookcase and is about to hide himself somewhere else. (On the wall of the room are pictures of John Lindsay, Martin Luther King, Franklin D. Roosevelt, and Napoleon. "My heroes," Woody said with a grin as the mixer played the scene for a rehearsal.) But before he goes he tells Diane that she has to get to the underground and tell them some vital information. It is one of his favorite exchanges of dialogue in the film.

WOODY

(*frantically*) The Aires Project. You remember that now?

DIANE

Yes. The Jupiter Project.

The scene played and Woody shook his head. "She says that right to my face. It's so blatantly stupid and yet it doesn't get a laugh."

After about a dozen times through, Woody and Ralph agreed on how loud the police sirens should be and when the policemen's footsteps should start and how loud Woody's and Diane's voices should be. But they didn't like the voice of the policeman outside announcing over a bullhorn that the premises were surrounded. So they looked at the only other person in the room and asked him to try the lines in the recording studio downstairs. He did and sounded at least better than what they had. The lines were cut in and they moved on to the next scene.

During a break Woody talked about how much he liked a book that had just come out on Walt Disney with pictures from all his films in it. "Disney is so representative of a certain style of the early forties. He has a style as pronounced as El Greco, say. He was experimenting in

140

deep water. The complicated backgrounds in the animated films make the figures in front more intricate. The backgrounds are as good as any of the sets designed for Broadway by Jo Mielziner. He had those intricate, complicated camera shots. The opening scene in *Pinocchio*, for instance, when the camera is on the city at night—it's like a helicopter shot. I really like American things: American food, music, Disney."

The mix for *Sleeper* ran perilously close to the day the film had to be sent out to be copied, and Grossberg and United Artists executives were especially worried. To add to the general anxiety over whether the film would be ready, Woody had gotten into his usual tug-of-war with UA over the publicity—something that happens with every film. Woody technically has approval of how the advertising is done in New York and Los Angeles, but not for the rest of the country. UA wanted to have a teaser (a non-action film of still photos of Woody and Diane) and a trailer (a longer, interview-format film of Woody interspersed with appropriate cuts from *Sleeper*). But UA's ideas and Woody's seldom match at first and there is a lot of tense—if friendly—fighting that goes on until an agreement is reached.

After weeks of arguing, UA had come up with a teaser and a trailer that they thought Woody would approve, and seven people from the UA ad department, including Gabe Sumner, the vice-president in charge of publicity, all showed up at the mix with the two films to show Woody. They looked like something out of *The Godfather* as they walked in together and made nervous jokes. They all sat down on one side of the room. Woody was alone on the other side. It resembled a shoot-out. The projectionist rolled the films. Woody approved them, with one very minor change. The UA contingent jumped up as a group, all smiles, and left before he could change his mind. Three of them lit cigars. The UA people and Woody each claim that they have nothing but the highest respect and regard and liking for each other, and it certainly seems as if they do. But they also make each other nervous, and while Woody may justly feel ganged up on when he alone has to face seven of them, he is by himself enough to visibly unsettle those seven.

"Advertising a Woody Allen film is very much like trying to commit suicide with a laugh and a smile and a song," Sumner had said some months earlier. "Woody says he doesn't really want us to advertise, to publicize, and he hates us to exploit. But the truth is that he really does want us to advertise, to publicize, and more than anything else exploit—but on his terms. He is insecure over what his image is and should be. Maybe that is good. It theoretically leaves us wide open as to what we're going to do with his films each time out.

"But Woody has very specific and dogmatic tastes in advertising. In print they run from white space and simplicity to more white space and utter simplicity. Woody gets ill even at the suggestion of a print campaign that may have lots of people doing lots of funny things to other people. We showed him the campaign for *Sex*. [It read: "You haven't seen everything until you've seen Everything," and underneath it had a composite cartoon of everyone in the cast wearing various costumes.] He got ill. We revived him. We've come to an understanding. We do two campaigns. One that he sees in New York and L.A. [The ad for *Sex* in those cities had a picture of Woody and

142

a picture of the book: "If you want to know how this man made a movie of this book, you'll have to see the movie."] and one that the rest of the country sees. We did that on *Sex*. We checked to see when he played Vegas and planned the releases accordingly.

"Yet he is extremely receptive to strange, weird, often exciting ideas. He stimulates us to do strange and weird and often more unusual things than we would normally do if it weren't for his great interest in these things.

"The radio, TV, and coming-attractions campaigns always please him easily. There is a greater flexibility with films and broadcast than there is with print. As long as it is all rightly focused on him, he's easy to get along with. He's *always* easy to get along with; pleasant and a lot of fun. But at times he's frustrating because he won't get red-faced or raise his voice. He comes in off the elevator looking like a messenger company reject, and he will lean on you, lean on you, then come back and do it ten times more until you either give in to him or die. ["Funny, that's the way I feel about them," Woody says.]

"I look forward to merchandising sessions with him more than any other creator in the business, knowing the obstacles and challenge he's going to give us. He's so stimulating. He has a well-conceived notion of what we *shouldn't* do. He's frank in that he doesn't care what the people out there think, what will motivate them to come. He hasn't yet sold out to what to do to get an extra buck. He has his own aesthetics and they shouldn't be offended.

"People have been told all sorts of things about *Sleeper*. One is that it is the story of a dwarf falling asleep under a tree. Technically, he has the right of consultation in advertising, not approval. But that is contract talk. The

143

fact is, he has the right of approval." Sumner gives a little laugh when he says that. It seems clear that as in everything else he does, though he does not act belligerently, Woody does not move until things are the way he likes them. "I guess it will turn out that Woody is an advertising genius like he is in every way. His unarticulated theories of advertising will be the rule of thumb. I hope this gives you an idea of how you have to ice skate with him to stay on the same lake."

With the problem of advertising *Sleeper* behind him, Woody was left with finishing up the final touches in time to get the picture into the theater. For *Sex* he was literally working on the final print until an hour before it opened at the Little Carnegie theater in New York, two doors down the street from the Rollins and Joffe offices where he edited it. But *Sleeper* had to have 350 copies made of it, and that takes at least a week.

Before a film can be sent off and duplicated, the color has to be corrected in it. This is done by a technician looking at the film and assigning a printing light to every scene; every time there is a light change—every cut—a new printing light is decided on and it is given a number that is measured in light density and color quality. The film is put through a machine that has the printing lights keyed in it and a print, called an answer print, is made and sent to the director to look at. The director then notes where he finds the light too soft or too harsh, or the color too blue, or green, or yellow, or whatever, and the technician reassigns numbers, trying to match what the director wants, and a corrected answer print is produced. A problem for *Sleeper* was that the lab was in Los Angeles and Woody and Ralph Rosenblum were watching the film in

144

New York, so every time they wanted a change—and it turned out there were more than a half-dozen corrected answer prints that had to be made—the film had to go back to Los Angeles and more time was lost.

Woody sat down one morning to watch what he hoped would be a perfect print. "This may be the last time I ever have to see this movie in my life," he said hopefully. It wasn't. Several more prints followed. Everyone got nervous. They tried showing the film in the two theaters in New York where it was going to open to see how it looked there. Not great. More answer prints. In one theater they looked green, in another, yellow. No matter how uniform they are supposed to be, different lights in different projectors in different theaters give different images.

Finally, with a couple of days left, the print was as corrected as it was going to get. *Sleeper,* after a year's work, was ready to be released. Woody saw the film for probably the last time in his life and went home to work on a new play—and to see what the response would be to *Sleeper.*

It was Ralph Rosenblum who summed up what all the work had come down to. It wasn't with audiences or critics that the fate of the film really lay. "This is a multi-million-dollar industry," he said after the last screening which, because it was in a different theater, looked different from the one before it. "This is a multi-million-dollar industry and it finally funnels down to an Italian or Jewish projectionist reading the *Daily News* while the manager buzzes up saying, 'Hey, Eddie, focus it.'"

8.
"You have to end like a house afire."

There is an implicit agreement between the maker of a comedy and his audience, and it is that the ending will be funny and, in a way, pleasing. In drama, the ending can be tragic, bittersweet, pathetic, heartwarming, optimistic, even upsetting; in short, so long as it somehow can follow out of the story, it can fall anywhere within the range of human emotion. The options for endings in comedy are limited, yet in comedy, perhaps more than in any other kind of film, a good ending is crucial. A particular problem of Woody's is finding appropriate endings for his films.

"As you get on in a script to the final half hour, you have to be more and more funny," he says. "You have to accelerate and keep the pace up and end like a house afire. You can joke around with the audience through the movie, but you have to wrap it up so they are amused or satisfied.

146

It just can't be a joke or too abrupt. The ending has a larger effect. It can help or hurt you retroactively. It has added impact."

The problem with Woody's films is that they are filled with a lot of surprises, non sequiturs, and abrupt bouncing around from one thing to another. His stories are odd. They are not conventional stories told in conventional ways, so the endings don't automatically come out of the material that precedes them. (The ending to *Play It Again, Sam* is the most satisfying of his films because its story is the most conventional and contiguous; the ending is a logical extension.)

In every film, Woody tries more than one ending. In *Take the Money and Run* he tried several. In one, Virgil Starkwell, the bank robber (Woody) is shot and buried. After the funeral his wife and child are standing by the grave. As they start to walk away, Virgil's voice says, "Come back tonight with a shovel and we'll go away with the money." "Gee," his wife says to the boy, "for a minute there I thought I heard your father's voice." In another, Virgil is shot on the street and covered with a sheet. His glasses, which all through the film have been deliberately stepped on by various menacing and hostile people, are by his side. As a policeman goes over to stomp on them as everyone else has, Virgil's hand shoots out from under the sheet and grabs them. The ending Woody finally used has Virgil back in prison.

NARRATOR
Virgil Starkwell is tried on fifty-two counts of robbery and sentenced to eight hundred years in federal prison.

At the trial he tells his lawyer confidently that with good behavior he can cut his sentence in half.

NARRATOR
(now speaking with Virgil) Virgil, now that you're caught and you're facing a very long prison sentence, do you have any regrets about choosing a life of crime?

VIRGIL
I think crime definitely pays and that, uh, you know, it's a great . . . the hours are good, and you're your own boss, and you travel a lot, and you . . . you get to meet interesting people and . . . uh . . . I just think it's a good job in general.

NARRATOR
What about your cohorts. What ever happened to them? All the guys you've been associated with in various gangs.

VIRGIL
A great many of them have . . . uh . . . become . . . uh . . . homosexuals, and some of them have entered into politics and sports.

NARRATOR
Well, how do you manage to spend your time in prison? Do you have any hobbies or anything?

148

VIRGIL

I do. I . . . I . . . I've been working on
. . . I've been doing a lot of stuff in the
shop, actually, and . . . uh . . . I . . . I'm
very skilled with my hands. I . . . uh
. . . do you know if it's raining out?

The original ending to *Sleeper* had Miles Monroe
(Woody), Luna (Diane Keaton), and Erno, the underground leader who overthrows the government mainly
by their help, driving in a car.

ERNO

By tomorrow morning our forces will
control all the vital positions necessary
for a takeover. *(beat)* Darling, I was so
worried about you.

LUNA

I'm fine.

MILES

Take it easy. She loves me.

ERNO

Is that true?

LUNA

Of course not.

MILES

Really?

ERNO

I'm sorry Miles.

MILES

Okay—let me out.

149

LUNA

What?

MILES

You heard me. Pull over.

Car screeches to a halt.

ERNO

Don't be angry—I'm charismatic.

LUNA

Where are you going?

MILES

There's going to be a new world. From
now on I'm on my own.

LUNA

Miles. . . .

MILES

See you in the next life.

*Camera stays with Miles. We hear car stopping. Sound of
door slamming. We hear footsteps—music—as Miles
turns to Erno.*

MILES

What the hell do you want?

ERNO

She wants you.

Miles turns to car and gets in.

LUNA

Don't ask me why—I'm attracted to
you—I must be sick.

*They kiss. Miles and Luna drive off. In the background a
gigantic chicken from earlier in the film is chasing Erno.*

150

In the ending that was used, Miles also wins Luna. They drive down the road with Miles professing his disbelief in politics, science, love, religion—in fact, everything but "sex and death. Two things that happen to me only once in my life. Only after death you're not nauseous."

The worst trouble with an ending, though, was a sequence for *Everything You Always Wanted to Know About Sex*, and it is illustrative of a number of things about Woody and his work. The segment was titled *"What Makes a Man a Homosexual?"* and Woody and Louise Lasser played in it—Woody as a common spider, Louise as a black widow. (It was not included in the finished film.)

"I was coming out of the optician's on Lexington Avenue and Seventy-Seventh Street," Woody recalls, "and the spider sequence suddenly hit me. At that moment I had no ending for it. I just thought it was a great idea that I was a spider and there would be a black widow and we would have sex and she would devour me and that would symbolically show one reason why men become homosexuals. I thought it was so great and theatrical. I wanted to get Louise because she's great at improvising. I was sure we would come up with an ending between then and the time I shot it."

A huge web was constructed on the sound stage from steel cables, two spider costumes with long legs and humps on the back were designed and made, and Louise and Woody, who hates costumes anyway but hated this one the most, suited up.

Before Louise went over to the web and struggled up to the middle of it, she turned to Woody. "Should I call

151

myself Adelle Fleigleman? Do you have a name in mind?"
she asked.

"Lisa," Woody answered.

"Well, would Adelle Fleigleman be all right? I'd hate to
cast myself."

"Anything would be all right as long as it gets a laugh."

"You know, all the girls you name are either Lisa or
Nancy."

"Yes, well, I can type them in a hurry."

"And they all have the same birthday."

A camera was set up way in the top of the sound stage
and a piece of cardboard with a small hole in it was put
over the lens to make a long, tight shot. Another camera
was set up to record Woody on the floor at the beginning
of the scene, and they shot it. And they shot it again. And
again. They shot it through the three days it was supposed
to take, through a week, through nearly two weeks. There
was still no appropriate ending.

During a break after about a week of shooting, Woody
and Louise were talking in the little dressing room that
was on the sound stage.

"I can't take any more of this," he complained. "I'm
going to have a nervous breakdown. I hate my life."

"You could be here alone," Louise said.

"It's so *hard*," he moaned.

After giving up hope of finishing the sequence in Los
Angeles, a portion of the web was brought back to New
York, where additional attempts requiring only a camera-
man and sound man instead of a crew of fifty were made.
A suitable ending was never found.

The sequence, as written, follows. In their attempt to

make it work, Woody and Louise tried a great many variations on the lines, but their flavor, and that of the sequence, was unchanged. While the concept is funny, the lines are improved by visualization and thus would be better seen on film. Still, the sequence gives a rather good idea of Woody's troubles in finding the right ending to a comic concept.

Open on shot of what at first looks like some strands of filament but gradually we discern it to be a large spider web.

Camera drifting over to center of web and we discover an enormous black widow spider, that is, a seductive woman in a large spider costume with eight legs and an hourglass figure on her belly. Her arms and legs form four legs and four legs are part of the costume.

She is very sexy and is combing her long black hair, or long blonde hair, depending.

Camera drifts down to bottom of web (and it may be that the web is constructed in such a way that shooting it from the proper angle, such as above, or camera on its side, can give us a sense of antigravity).

Anyhow, along floor, not on web, comes crawling a much smaller male spider played by me. Black body, eight legs, glasses, etc.

The spider notices the sexy oversized woman at web center.

WOODY

Hey, look at her . . . she's dynamite.
. . . I could never score with someone

like that. . . . Jesus, will you look at her.
. . . Oh, I'd like to do it to her. . . . Walk
by again. . . . Maybe she'll notice . . .
and try to be casual. . . .

He does his funny spider walk past her, trying to be casual.

Cut to: FEMALE
Primping, combing hair, looking seductive.

WOODY
She's playing it cool. . . . I better go into
my mating dance. . . . that'll get her.
. . . I'm so sexy during my mating
dance. . . . Ahem! Hello—

FEMALE
Hello.

WOODY
Nice day, isn't it?

FEMALE
Yes.

WOODY
O.K., she's looking, now the mating
dance, you'll drive her wild. . . .

*He goes into his "instinct" mating dance. A preposterous
series of gyrations, hopefully sexual to another spider but
kind of absurd.*

Finally he is pooped.

WOODY
This is ridiculous. . . . I'm getting no-
where. . . . Why don't you just talk to
her . . . go ahead . . . don't be shy.
. . . Hello.

154

FEMALE

Hello.

WOODY

Nice day, isn't it?

FEMALE

Um.

WOODY

What's your name?

FEMALE

Lisa. What's yours?

WOODY

Sheldon Wexler.

FEMALE

What do you do?

WOODY

I'm a spider. *(to himself)* Jesus, what a
jerky thing to say.

FEMALE

I know you're a spider. You just seem
er . . . lost.

WOODY

I'm OK. I . . . er . . . you're a black
widow, eh?

FEMALE

Yeah. I'd ask you in but you look busy.

WOODY

Busy? Me? No, I'm not due home till
eight-thirty. Mother's making me a little piece of sugar for dinner.

FEMALE

Well, would you like to come in?

155

WOODY
I'd love to. *(to himself)* Now don't
blow it because you can score and
she's a doll.

*Shot of Woody delicately negotiating the strands of web.
We should be able to get some good shots here between the
natural slapstick of it and placing the camera at gravity-
defying angles.*

WOODY
You'll have to forgive me, I'm a little
tired from my mating dance.

FEMALE
Is that what that was? I thought you
were having a convulsion.

WOODY
(forcing laugh) Ha, ha . . . right. . . .

*He manages to enter web, part way up. The two sit in
insectlike juxtaposition.*

WOODY
It's a very nice web you got here. Live
alone?

FEMALE
Yes.

*At this news, Woody shudders with excitement like a bad
comic.*

WOODY
Dd-di-zing—score-score. . . .

FEMALE
Where's your web?

WOODY
138th Street and Lenox Avenue.

156

FEMALE

So what are you doing in the Village?

WOODY

I was out walking. I accidentally got into a taxicab.

FEMALE

Oh—it's tough being an insect, we're always getting lost.

WOODY

I have a friend, Leo Braverman— maybe you know him—he's a flea—he was spending last winter on a collie. Nice animal. So the collie was feeding next to a spaniel and Leo looked over and saw a very attractive female flea just stretched out, sunbathing on the back of the spaniel—you know, un- aware that she was being spied at from a taller dog. Well, to make a long story short, Leo fell in love with her and paid her a little visit. But it didn't work out. Difference in temperaments. Leo has a tremendous temper for a flea. Anyhow, when Leo left to get back on his collie, the dog's owners had moved to Europe taking the dog with them. . . . The rest of the details are not im- portant. . . . Leo finally mounted a Mexican hairless and died of sunstroke during a hot August. . . .

FEMALE

That's a sad story.

WOODY

I just bring it up to show you how we insects always have our homes uprooted. . . . Fate is very cruel. . . .

FEMALE

Yes.

WOODY

Are you married?

FEMALE

I was married. My husband died.

WOODY

I'm sorry.

FEMALE

It's O.K. You adjust.

WOODY

You can adjust to anything. I knew a moth. Harvey Adelman—from Cleveland. . . . he could only eat heavy woolens and somehow he found himself in Arizona for his lungs. He found he could do very well with lighter fabrics and even leather. . . . I only bring it up. . . .

FEMALE

At times I am lonely.

WOODY

I understand. A beautiful, young spider like you.

FEMALE

You think I'm beautiful?

WOODY

I do. And I see a lot of stuff crawling around the floor.

FEMALE

Thank you.

WOODY

You have lovely legs.

FEMALE

Oh . . . I mean, I'm happy with five of them but the other three are overweight.

WOODY

No, you're earthy, buxom . . . that's very sexy.

FEMALE

Ooooh.

WOODY

What's the matter?

FEMALE

I'm a little stiff. My shoulder. I've been so tense lately.

WOODY

Can I help? You want a back rub?

FEMALE

A back rub? Would it be trouble?

WOODY

Not at all.

Goes to her and begins working on her back.

159

FEMALE

Gee, that feels good. You are strong.

WOODY

Well. . . .

FEMALE

I'll bet you're a real swinger . . . am I
right?

WOODY

*(starting to become confident that
she's open for a proposition)* I can go
pretty good. . . .

FEMALE

You probably do great with the
females. . . .

WOODY

Let's say—I get my share. . . .

FEMALE

Ever make it with a black widow
before?

WOODY

No . . . just your basic garden variety
spider. . . . I once went down on a bee
. . . we were kids. . . .

FEMALE

*(now she's breathing hotly on him and
taking control)* It's been so long since
I've done it with anyone.

WOODY

Poor thing.

FEMALE

You're not scared of me, are you?

WOODY

(trying to be tough) Are you kidding.
. . . *(kiss, begin to fondle)*

FEMALE

Oh, hold me, hold me—Oh, Sheldon. . . .

*Music swells and in a series of typically discreet camera
moves we see these two spiders trying to clumsily make it.
Gradually they do but we don't witness it as the camera
drifts in too close and dissolves to afterwards. They both
lie there staring. She is smoking a cigarette. Typical postcoital scene except they're spiders.*

WOODY

I feel good. Tired, but good.

FEMALE

Uh-huh.

WOODY

You were wonderful.

FEMALE

So were you.

WOODY

I mean it. Just great. . . . Well, I gotta
be going. . . . I'll come by again and
maybe we can even go for a walk.
. . . So long, kid.

FEMALE

(calmly) You're not going anyplace.

WOODY

What?

FEMALE

I'm going to devour you now.

161

WOODY

Pardon me?

FEMALE

You're not leaving the web, I'm going
to have you for dinner.

WOODY

It's a funny joke. Listen, I'll see you.

FEMALE

Sheldon, I'm not joking. I'm going to
devour you.

WOODY

Why don't you get some rest. I'm due
back at my own web. Ooops. . . .

He tries moving but finds it hard to negotiate the strands.
He flops clumsily this way and that.

WOODY

Hey, what is this?

FEMALE

You can't escape, Sheldon. Entering
the web is easy but leaving is another
matter.

WOODY

You're kidding about this.

FEMALE

You're going to be eaten, Sheldon.

WOODY

Why? Was I such a bad lay?

FEMALE

You were wonderful.

WOODY

So why are you getting hostile?

FEMALE

I'm not hostile. It's nature's way.

WOODY

(backing off) Screw nature. Boy, the women I get mixed up with!

Tries getting out but keeps falling.

FEMALE

You're not going to get away, Sheldon, the male never does.

WOODY

Don't come near me. This is no way to start a relationship.

She is chasing him now and the two are running all over the web, scrambling.

WOODY

If I knew you were going to carry on like this, I'd never have given you my body.

She's advancing and he's getting tangled up.

WOODY

Lisa, you're suffering from the worst postcoital depression I've ever seen! Lisa. . . .

She's putting filament on him, putting him into a cocoon-type covering.

FEMALE

That's the way it is with the black widow. Sex with the male and then he appears on the menu.

WOODY

When word of this gets out, you're going to have a lot of trouble getting
dates! Lisa! Lisa! Lisa!

*As she has him trapped fatally, the camera zooms back
throwing the scene into the distance and revealing
Woody as a regular professor of entomology, looking into
a microscope.*

*We understand he's been watching this scene in his office
lab.*

*Presently, his secretary enters. The girl who was the black
widow.*

SECRETARY

Dr. Hall, I finished all the typing. Can
I leave because my husband is picking
me up? We have theater tickets.

WOODY

(speaks like a homosexual) Oh, sure,
sweetheart, go ahead, have a very
good time and I'll see you here tomorrow. 'Night.

"It never had an ending and it never went anyplace,"
Woody said of the sequence two years after it was filmed.
"The thing that was wrong with it in the first five seconds
that I thought of it remained wrong right through. You
think you'd be able to get a three-minute sequence out of
that. It was one of the most hateful experiences of my life.
If I could have gotten any kind of ending I would have left
it in.

"But it's a perfect example of where just with *Sleeper*

I began to see that audiences want to see me in movies. I opted for the transvestite sequence with Lou Jacobi instead of it, based on the fact that I thought I was in too many sequences and why put in another one if I'm not particularly sure of it. But the audience comes to see me. People said, 'You should have been in all the sequences,' but I couldn't conceive of that. I could have played them all, like the one with Gene Wilder—though maybe not as well—but I could have played a guy in love with a sheep. It is the same sort of reticence I had with my band when I started playing with them. I couldn't be the leader."

9.
"What I'm trying to do is grow."

"My feelings have always been that when you're not sure of what you have, you want to see what the reviews are, as I did with *Don't Drink the Water* and *Take the Money and Run;* or if you think you've done badly you want to see if maybe you weren't so bad," Woody says. "But when you as an artist know a thing is good, everything else is irrelevant. If you know in your heart it's good and you didn't goof it, and they say it's no good, then they're wrong and who cares? Otherwise, you make yourself crazy."

Even though Woody pays fleeting attention to critics, he still is very aware of them. He does read most of what is written about his work, if only because he reads the publications they appear in. While he is his own severest critic and pays far more attention to what he thinks about his efforts than what anyone else thinks, he certainly is not

166

deaf to suggestions from people he trusts. He is also friendly with several critics and on occasion he speaks at film- and theater-related programs or workshops that they are involved in.

One of these was a weekend seminar on his films that *New York* Magazine film critic Judith Crist was running at a conference center in Tarrytown, about forty minutes north of New York City. On the way up in the limousine provided by the seminar, Woody listened to a New York Knicks game, wishing over and over that he was watching it at Madison Square Garden, where he has season tickets. He was not in a good mood: in addition to missing the Knicks game, he had seen Bergman's *The Seventh Seal* the day before and *Cries and Whispers* that day. "I see his films and I wonder what I'm doing."

Woody has been very fortunate as far as criticism of his work goes, and he acknowledges and appreciates both the power of the critics and the fact that they "have been in my corner overwhelmingly in every medium, for the most part. They've been generous with me. They've chosen to emphasize my good points rather than my weak points most of the time. They've encouraged me for the most part and I think that's good, because to use a terrible metaphor, you're a weak flower at the beginning and you're poking your head up over the soil and they can chop it off. You have no defenses. Still, their value is strictly economic. They can hurt your picture sometimes; sometimes they can't do that. They can't do anything for you as an artist, for or against. If they say you're bad, it doesn't mean you're bad. If they say you're good, it doesn't mean you're good. I think if there were no critics there wouldn't be the slightest scintilla of impairment of

167

art. The true artists have no connection with them and do their work. I don't have contempt for critics or anything. It's just that artists do all they know how to do. Bergman or Truffaut can make a film and you can criticize it fifty million ways. But all they can do is make their own kind of films.

"People who are not venal should not be subject to criticism. Lots of directors are not out to make the big exploitative bucks—people like Antonioni, Bergman, Altman, Truffaut, Penn"—he laughed—"and me. Just the producers who are out to make the big exploitative bucks. If I were making films like *Lost Horizon,* where I pick something deliberately and milksop it up deliberately and try every sleazy trick to bring customers in, then I think I would be open to criticism, and legitimately so.

"But when Antonioni makes *Zabriskie Point,* which I liked, and it's a critical and commercial failure—all right, we understand that. But the guy wants to be free to work and not be worried about a swarm of gnats hovering over all the time. Who needs that? Again, it doesn't bother you personally so much. But filmmakers are always involved in financial tension and crisis. It's always hard to get money for films, and you're dealing with corporations whose business is money, and you've got a fight on your hands. It's not helpful to a guy like Fellini or Antonioni or Altman or Truffaut. We should say, no matter what happens to guys like that, they've proven that they're responsible, well-meaning men with talent, that they should work all the time, that they should never have any problems with having their work insulted when it fails."

Woody's opinions are arguably more altruistic than self-serving. It was true when he was saying this, and it is true now, that he could walk into any studio and get the picture deal he wanted with no trouble. At that point, in fact, United Artists was in the process of offering him a contract for another five pictures and giving him total artistic freedom—a deal he ultimately accepted.

There were still a few minutes left in the Knicks game when the car arrived where the seminar was taking place, so Woody listened on until he was sure the Knicks had it wrapped up, then he went inside. The director of the center greeted him and took him to a side room with a piano in it where they waited for Ms. Crist. Woody went over to the piano and picked out several bars of " 'Round Midnight."

"How do you like being in the country?" he was asked.

"Like in *On the Waterfront*—'The crickets make me nervous.' That pretty well sums it up. I have an attack of agraphobia when I go to the country. I feel like I'm going to come down with some disease unknown to everyone except a special New York doctor."

To guard against possible attack, he had in his overcoat pockets: Compazine, Darvon, Lomotil, Valium, a tooth brush, a tin of Sucrets, a package of Luden's cough drops, and a book on four existential theologians.

Later he talked some more about critics. "When I come out with a picture, I don't pore over reviews. Sometimes something special will interest me, like the French reviews of *Sex*. When I say I couldn't care less about the reviews, it's because there's nothing I can do about it. If that's the way they feel, I'm certainly not going to change my style of comedy if they don't like it, or pander to a certain group if they do like it. United Artists feels that the press has made heroes of critics by putting their quotes on

169

ads. But I think that's totally within the province of advertising. If I do a film and a critic says it is a charming and funny comedy, my inclination would be to use that in the advertisement. It's strictly a question then of trying to coax people to go and see it. And in the end, you can only coax people to go and see it for a couple of weeks, because then the criticism is totally forgotten and word of mouth takes over. The picture either has something that people respond to or it doesn't.

"I've often had the feeling, 'Gee, why don't they leave me alone and let me work.' My intent is not venal. I'm not trying to make formula pictures that are going to trade on pandering to people's worst instincts. I'm trying to make original comedies, some of which will succeed, some of which will fail, some of which will do both in the same film —some have. You don't want to be bothered and nit-picked and under the gun all the time. You want to work and that's it."

Yet he does try to learn selectively from criticism of his work. An example of how he tries to get something from a critic he has "great affection and respect for" came after *Sleeper* was released and Pauline Kael published in *The New Yorker* the lengthiest review the film received. Woody read it carefully and a couple of times brought up points it raised while talking with Jack Rollins about possible ideas for his next film. It was one of Kael's contentions that Woody lacked a supporting cast with character, that he tended to be a loner at all times.

"I think it is true that if I made the film more complex, giving more character to other parts would work," he said after considering the piece. "It's a problem. Vincent Canby had the most incisive review of *Take the Money* in

170

that it *was* a visual monologue. I've always had a tendency to play the clarinet alone, to do everything alone. I gave Diane a certain amount of character in *Sleeper* but it was an afterthought. One thing to be remembered is that I'm being reviewed in the present and films like the Marx Brothers' are past. Fifty years from now [my films] will have a different quality entirely and critics will be criticizing some young film comedian and saying, 'What Woody Allen always seemed to have was a good command of the . . .' you know. In the end, that's really a very important thing. In time you pass into the pantheon. Some of the best Buster Keaton films, he's alone. He's got a girl friend with some character to her, but not much, and some other characters come in and drop off."

The biggest point that Kael raised was that although *Sleeper* was the most consistent of Woody's films, it lacked "the wildman's indifference to everything but the joke."

Woody has thought about that. "It may turn out that I can make only surreal movies that are indifferent to everything but the joke. That is a possibility. I know that I could do a funnier comedy under certain circumstances if it's pure laughter. But the point is, I try not to do that, even if some of my films fail, because I know that I can always make crazy movies where I'm indifferent to everything but the joke, and I think that I can make them better and better. But I think that it would be a mistake to make only that kind of movie. It may be totally correct that as I start to make other types of comedies that I'm not working toward my strength. But it's too early for me to take the position that I can do only one kind of movie.

"What I have to do is make several movies that are different, that may not be so funny, that may fail, and then

171

look up and say, 'I really am only at fifty percent effective-
ness in anything except a crazy movie.' I hope that's not
true but it's possible. I know that if I wanted to play it safe
I could make a film full of wild, crazy laughs, and what I'm
trying to do is grow beyond that. If I lock into a style, what
will happen to me is what happened to the Marx Brothers.
They made in one sense, for better or worse, the same
movie over and over again. Whether it was *Go West* or
A Night at the Opera or *The Big Store*, it was always the
same movie. They were incredibly funny, so you happily
sat through it with them all the time because it was fun.

"What happens with a more serious artist, like Chaplin,
is you try to do other things. You don't go to your strength
all the time. And you strike out so people think you're an
ass or pretentious, but that's the only thing you can do.
You can find your groove and stay in it, and I think you
will inevitably fail a little if you don't stay in it. My only
disagreement with these people who are not as turned on
by *Sleeper* as my other films is that I think some of the
scenes in the movie—like the robot Jewish tailors—were
as absurd as any I've written."

After the success of *Sleeper*, Woody spent a lot of time
trying to decide what his next film would be. Mickey Rose,
who co-authored *Take the Money and Run* and *Bananas*,
came to New York in January 1974 and the two of them
threw ideas at each other over a period of weeks. Woody,
meanwhile, was working on a more serious idea, and he
expected that one film or the other would be shot in New
York at the beginning of the summer.

But he decided against both scripts and wrote a third,
which he was initially enthusiastic about. That enthusiasm

172

soon died. By June, when he was supposed to have begun filming, he still did not have a script he liked enough to go ahead with.

"I wanted to do a deeper comedy," he explained one day in mid-June. "I wanted to do a more human film—comedy but real person. Not a guy wakes up in the future, or a guy is a bank robber, or a guy takes over a Latin American country. I wanted to do one where I play me, Diane plays her, we live in New York. Conflict but real, as opposed to too flamboyant an idea.

"It's very tough, though. You can't believe the problems I encounter because of the particularness of my situation, because I'm not an actor; I'm not going to write a story where I play a southern sheriff. I'm always going to play me. And I'm believable as me only as certain things—as an urban little person my age. I would not be believable as a garbage man in New York. People expect me to say amusing things; that's what they're paying for. So that rules out many ideas. I've got to get an idea that's believable, yet funny and within my range.

"So you need a comedy about a big-city kind of person like myself. And there are very few big crises that one can believably get into. I don't want to get into murders. I don't want to get into spies or stuff like that, because that's all unbelievable and less human.

"So I wrote this idea, and I reread it, and I didn't like it. I liked the first half but not the second half. So then I rewrote. I got a completely new idea and used much of the first half that I liked, and I didn't like that. Then I got a third idea, which became further out, and I used much of the first half that I liked, and that didn't work for me either. So I've finished three things and now I'm kicking

173

around ideas. I've finished about thirty-eight pages of a new idea called *Love and Death*, that is very funny— funny in the sense that one reads an S.J. Perelman essay. It's just crazy, maniacally funny. It would be very good for Bob Hope. It's been one of the most pleasurable experiences in that sense; I've just got scenes one after the other there that Bob Hope should be doing; it would be a better movie than if I did it. But the problem is this: *Love and Death* is easy for me because it's flamboyant, it's not real at all. It's very funny in that crazy way. But I don't know yet if I'll complete it. I keep working a couple of pages a day on it and then take a few hours and try for another idea. I don't know if I'm doing the right thing or not in the sense that I might write a real story and people will come and they'll laugh at it but I'll get the same kind of reactions in certain quarters that I got with *Sam:* 'Yeah, I expected more far-out stuff, more imaginative stuff'; whereas the thing I'm working on fits right into the type of film people expect of me.

"Knowing that I am going to work with Keaton, at one time I was thinking about those type of things that Tracy and Hepburn did, because that would be fun. The problem, though, is Keaton and I are not Hepburn and Tracy. Our chemistry is completely different; theirs can't be duplicated. And times have changed. You see their films as old movies, so they're delightful. But they're plotty and based on standards that don't apply today.

"Modern stuff is very non-plotty, and plot is dynamite in comedy. When you're doing the kind of comedy like *Bananas* that doesn't have a plot, you've got a lot of problems and you're dependent on really tour-de-force things. You've got to be hilarious from the starting position and

174

hilarious again, and an hour goes by with no real plot and you're not getting any payoff from stuff you planted an hour ago; you're always in the starting position and you've got to be six times as funny at the end. Whereas, you get a premise going, a story—at the end you're cashing in on the relationships you've set up.

"All the accepted forms are great for comedy; that's why the comedians work in them so much. That's why a comedy mystery is a great idea, comedy science fiction, comedy Western. Those are all accepted forms, and if you see Hope, he'll be doing *Monsieur Beaucaire* or *Paleface* or *My Favorite Brunette,* and the same thing with Jerry Lewis. But if you try to do character comedy where you're dependent more on people's neuroses and less on plot, it's tough. Although I don't take it remotely seriously as I do, say, a Shaw play, *Sam* was a character comedy. The laughs didn't come from plotting. They came from the unfolding of a highly neurotic, bizarre personality caught in a situation, but in no way a plot like *Some Like It Hot* or *Adam's Rib.*

"You want to do it real nowadays: For example, in a plot this girl wants to live with me but she also wants to keep her own apartment as a psychological symbol of her independence. Those kinds of conflict are interesting and are how we've learned to better understand people, to try to analyze their behavior, or at least be aware that the conflicts are internal, because we're living in a psychoanalytic era and things don't appear to be as black and white as they used to be. And it's very tough to work funny conflict into that. Talk comedies were always about an external thing. It's very hard to get enough sparks going between the people. If Diane and I were to argue in a movie, to do

175

it realistically it would have to be about internal, psychological things. You can see the old example of it perfectly in 'I Love Lucy.' They created a conflict every week, something like her wanting to get into show business and disguising herself as the bongo player, that external kind of conflict; that's why it's called a situation comedy.

"*Born Yesterday* is a play that's right on the line perfectly. It's real, about an intelligent problem, it's got a good message, very respectable for a comedy (a comedy with any message is welcome), fresh characters who are real and just short of cartooning. I can't think of another comedy that's right on the head like that. Naturally an audience is going to rock with laughter at *A Night at the Opera* or *Duck Soup*—comedy of that type where your tacit contract at the beginning is, 'Listen, don't take me seriously, I'm just going to pull out all the stops and make you guys laugh.' There are no heights he wouldn't go to or depths he wouldn't sink to to make us laugh, and it's all crazy time, and it's a particular type of feeling. But then there's that other type of feeling where you see a movie and you *feel* in addition—it just doesn't appeal to you through the mind. You know, the character calls for the girl and he's very funny waiting in the rain in front of her house, and it's hilarious. But even though it is in no way sentimental it's also got some feeling to it. You would like him to meet her.

"And most people have trouble with conceptual comic ideas, too. I come up with a conception like an immense breast, or whatever, and they have trouble with the concept. They find it hard to stand back and say, 'My God, what a funny concept that is. An enormous breast. It's so

176

ridiculous.' They laugh joke by joke within it, which is the problem. You say the concept in one line but to show it you ultimately have to proceed joke by joke. You still wind up having to do a million jokes. People don't say, 'What a funny idea!' They say, 'Yeah, an immense breast. What's the joke?' "

By July Woody had decided on *Love and Death* as his next film. But instead of shooting it in New York, as he had originally intended with his earlier ideas, plans were being made to shoot in Paris, Hungary, Yugoslavia, or a combination of the three. Woody spent a couple of days sitting in an office at Marian Dougherty Associates, who were casting the film, looking over possible actors. In between appointments—there were close to a hundred in two days, each of five minutes or less duration—Fred Gallo occasionally popped in with various forms that needed Woody's signature. One time it was visa applications.

" 'S.F.R.J.' What's that?" he asked Gallo.

"Yugoslavia."

"Yugo*sla*via? Jesus. Occupation . . . writer. Purpose of trip . . . overthrow the government."

Gallo left after reminding Woody that he was due at Rockefeller Center to have his visa photos taken at three o'clock. Woody finished and walked the twenty blocks, crossing the street when necessary to have a better angle on approaching women he found attractive.

After making a quick weekend trip to Los Angeles to have two days of intensive French with his teacher, he took off for Paris to find locations. With some effort it was decided that almost all the film could be shot in and around Paris, a city he enjoys, rather than having to spend seven months in Zagreb or Budapest, a possibility that left him pale.

As usual the first day of shooting was a disaster, but he fell less behind than normal. One morning, however, he was standing under a tree on a cold day while a shot was being set up. He had spent the last several days filming some elaborate scenes involving two boys who were supposed to be Woody's character at ages seven and twelve, and finally he was working on some other scenes. He looked numb from more than the cold. He was.

"I came to a horrible realization a while ago," he said, shaking his head. "It's just one of those things that everyone misses. The French have an idea about the *auteur* being right and knowing what he's doing, so nobody thought much about it at the time, but I shot the wrong kid for three days. Those big scenes, I shot the wrong kid. I don't know what I'm going to do. They looked so good, and there were all those extras."

Lunchtime came and he went off to the tent in the field where lunch was ready and, after some hot chocolate and warming up a bit, he was more optimistic. He walked around, clapping his gloved hands.

"The ideas are moving around now. I think if I make a couple of shots to establish the kid I used and cut the scenes of the other one and write a couple of jokes that have to get laughs, I may be able to get away with it and the kids at the UCLA film school will think I know what I'm doing."

Since ultimately he relies only on his own judgment of what is good or bad about his work, Woody does not feel

178

that awards and prizes are valid. Thus he has moved quietly on the occasions he has been nominated for the awards the Writer's Guild gives for scripts to have his name removed from consideration. And, to his regret in one way, but not others, he rejects the notion that an Academy Award means anything.

"There are two things that bother me about them," he explained one day after Vincent Canby had asked in print why *Sleeper* had not been nominated for anything. "They're political and bought and negotiated for, and the whole concept of awards is silly. I cannot abide by the judgment of other people, because if you accept them when they say you deserve an award, then you have to accept them when they say you don't. It's *The Green Hills of Africa*, that's what it is. You put yourself in their hands as you're judged, and you're flattered, and the next year they say, 'No, you don't get it, Steve McQueen gets it'— and you know you were fantastic. The whole thing goes against everything you've worked for in your life.

"Also, there's no provision made for comedy and never has been. Consequently, artists like Groucho Marx and Charlie Chaplin and Buster Keaton never win Academy Awards. But it's not fair. Of course, if you're judging Groucho Marx against *Death of a Salesman* or *Streetcar Named Desire*, it's wrong. These guys are spectacular artists and they always get kind of stepson Oscars that are voted out of largesse, and that's not right. It bothers me. I wish it was different. I think it would be wonderful if the Academy Awards were truly a spectacular occasion and the awards meant something and glamorous people did them and it was really a step-out night.

"The only thing I regret about the Academy Awards is

that I can't perform on it. It kills me, because now I've been offered it. And it really bothers me because I know it's a big event and I know I could kill that audience because they're all show people. Sometimes I say to myself, 'Well, you don't even have to present one or accept one or get involved, but you can certainly perform on it, go out and do ten minutes and really break it up and you'll be seen by more people than will see your movies for the next twenty years.' But I can't bring myself to do it, and I'm such a logical choice for it, because I'm a comedian and I can MC and I'm in films. And then I say, 'Jane Fonda, who is great and whom I admire did it, and she's crabby about everything.' It kills me."

One reason it kills him is that Bob Hope—whom Woody adored when he was growing up—did it so well for so many years. One of his fantasies was to do the same. "I used to love Bob Hope on the Oscars; and I'd watch them still if he did it. Nobody could do those name jokes and MC like him. It was like the New York Yankees."

Woody does have one award that was given him; he is at a loss as to what to do with it other than keep it in a small closet in a back room under some old scripts. It was sent to him unannounced from "The Dating Game." Inscribed on it is: "Woody Allen, One of the World's Most Eligible Bachelors, 1973."

10.
Feeding the monster

Like chorus girls with silicone breasts, most comedians are supported by more than meets the eye. In the case of comedians, the support is gag writers—people who can come up with a funny line or routine that perfectly fits the comedian's style and character.

For keeping his comic funny, a good comedy writer commands enormous sums of money. In 1960, Woody was making $1,700 a week writing for Garry Moore. A good comedy writer can also engender enormous amounts of resentment from his comedian, because the comic realizes that without the writer, he is in trouble; his public persona is nurtured by this anonymous clever man.

"A comedian is not your garden variety-type person," says Larry Gelbart, who has worked for practically every great funnyman and is one of the best comedy writers around. "Given years of success or power, he's going to get more and more sort of bizarre. Jackie Gleason has moved whole networks to other parts of the Union because he wanted to broadcast from there. They have more power than is really good for them and they don't hesitate to use it. A lot of them have the feeling that for the money they're paying, you should stay the extra minute after work, or the whole night. You can become depersonalized. Years ago, for example, Norman Panama and Mel Frank were a writing team at MGM. One day Mel Frank was walking alone and [producer] Arthur Freed passed him. 'Hello, boys,' he said."

Comedy writing is a specialty; it is often a frustrating one. The fact that most shows are written not by one person but rather by a group sitting around throwing ideas and lines at one another can lessen the writer's self esteem.

"Suddenly we get the appellation 'writer,'" Mel Brooks said several years ago when he was solely a writer. " 'Written by Bing Bang . . .' and come to the old neighborhood and, 'Hey, you wrote that?' 'Yeah. . . .' I couldn't write on the back of a paper bag to figure out the numbers. You get the term writer and you're not really a writer, you're a screaming eighty-eight throwing shells into a mélange of sounds, hoping that your explosions will get closest to the target. You go home and you want to make the dream come true and you take a Mongol number two with a dull point, and you begin writing something that you hope will be a little more eloquent and a little more beautiful."

Or as Mel Tolkin once said, "Something else happens

182

personally to writers. Each one says, 'What am I doing? Do I call myself a writer?' I look at a sketch, and they tell you that was some swell sketch, and, all I know, I had one line in it. There are writers who make thousands of dollars who have almost never sat at a typewriter. What did they do? Well, you run around, somebody is at the typewriter, some little red-haired kid . . . he's the guy who writes the big play, he's the one guy who doesn't contribute much; he just puts all this childishness, yelling, and screaming into fairly good English."

Comedy writers often refer to their work as "feeding the monster," or the character of the comedian, and of the need to "housebreak" a comic so he respects the writer's individuality. Almost all of them dream of writing plays or films on their own, and a few, like Gelbart and Brooks and Neil Simon and Woody, succeed. Otherwise, Woody says, "Writing for people, you're a paid hack. That's what I was and what I could do to this day. You go in and ask them, 'What do you want?'— and then do it. There's nothing to doing that if you can do it. If I was going to write something for Gleason or Carney, it's dictated what is to be done. But writing for those anonymous nightclub comics who had no personality and never would have, they'd say, 'What should I talk about, what's my attitude? Should I get out there and be angry? Should I be a nebbish? Should I make phone calls to my mother?' I could never answer that. There is no answer, but at the time I didn't know that. The good comics establish a personality, like Hope, then get guys to feed that monster."

When Woody went to Hollywood in 1954 to "feed the

monsters," he had only written jokes and had no idea of how to develop ideas into a story line for a sketch. Fortunately, he started working with Danny Simon, who was one of the few writers who did. Woody was awestruck by Simon and Simon's interest in him: "I've learned a couple of things on my own since and modified things he taught me, but everything, unequivocally, that I learned about comedy writing I learned from him. When I started with Danny it was not so much a lack of discipline on my part as it was a total ignorance of what to do in every department. I was just a guy who knew how to make jokes and had funny ideas for things. It wasn't as though I was a writer with technique who lacked discipline. I lacked just the basic, simple knowledge of where to show up and start writing. After working with Danny I had stupefying confidence, and I've never lost it."

Simon taught Woody about plot construction and even influenced how he physically went about writing: he started writing on a typewriter and walking around the room doing the jokes out loud. Simon was careful about development and form, about talking over ideas and not starting to write until they were talked through and the direction of the sketch was known. They wrote sketches from the beginning and worked through to the end without jumping around. If a smashing joke came along but it took them from the mainstream of the plot, it was not used. "That used to kill me all the time," Woody says now, but it was one of the best lessons he learned—even if he doesn't always apply it. "I also learned that if I'm writing a scene that I'm not sure of in any way, I could act it out by myself in a room. If it works in a room, there's a good chance that it's going to work, because you're actually doing it. Danny took me out of fantasy and into reality. Suddenly I was in a situation where you had to come up with one or two sketches every week. You had to show up in the morning and *write* them. I mean, we were getting a lot of money and the stuff had to be delivered."

Later, when Woody was living in New York and freelance writing for comics, "Danny would call me from a phone booth when he was in town and say, 'Hey, I've got a great thing for you to work on,' and have me meet him in a pouring rain someplace, and he would always secretly tell me he thought he could get me onto a show. And he always would. A television writer's life was one where you picked up two weeks here and then that show folded." Among the people Woody wrote for on a more permanent basis were Peter Lind Hayes, Herb Shriner, Garry Moore, and Sid Caesar; the jobs for Caesar were the most enjoyable.

There was very little comedy from character on television when Woody wrote for it; it was practically all situational, and the situations were invariably the same, only fitted to a specific show—different versions of the jealous husband, the wife's old boy friend, or the husband's old girl friend; a pet in the attic or keeping a dog for a dear friend or perhaps finding a stray cat and taking it home.

"But today it's all emotional," Danny Simon says, "and I've been saying for years that action comes from emotion because I come from New York and the theater. Shows

185

today are based not on zaniness but on real characters, although somewhat exaggerated. Yet because of the personalities or the foibles or the character of these people themselves, you follow them emotionally. You very rarely see them go into what is called the big block comedy scene, like he's stuck in the closet—those are predicaments which used to be the big thing in the Gale Storm days of 'My Little Margie.' Today comedy comes from the peculiarity and patterns of that particular character, of that particular show, and they're not interchangeable. You very rarely will find a story that can be done on 'Sanford and Son' and on 'All In the Family' or 'The Mary Tyler Moore Show,' because they provoke their own original stories."

The one show in the middle and late 1950s that consistently had character jokes was Sid Caesar's "Your Show of Shows." Caesar acted every laugh—he *became* a Japanese movie star, if that's what the sketch was about—and the jokes were built on the believability of his satirization.

But even writing for Caesar had its drawbacks. While writers who worked on the show say that it raised them in their own estimation and made them rightly feel that they were a part of the best-written program around, there was still the problem of creativity by committee.

"At that point, you're not a writer, you're a trained, clever monkey," Larry Gelbart says. "When you can be a solo instrument, you feel much more the writer; in fact, you are. People say that Bob Hope, whom I used to write for, had thirteen writers at one time, but they never saw each other at once. They never knew which part of the

186

bomb they were building. As an indication of how crazy the staff system could be, there were something in the neighborhood of seventy-five writers who came and went while I was on 'Duffy's Tavern.' While it was a good show for writers, it was only a few who could last. Ideally, you get a situation where you work specials as I did and write with Sheldon Keller or Woody Allen."

Woody and Gelbart are alike in some ways. Both became big-time comedy writers while still in their teens (Gelbart is about ten years older than Woody). Both have gone beyond TV writing (Gelbart wrote *The Notorious Landlady*, co-authored *A Funny Thing Happened on the Way to the Forum*, and is co-producer of the "M*A*S*H" television series, which he adapted for TV), both are fierce about maintaining their individuality, and they share a comic sensibility.

They met in 1959 when Gelbart was working for Sid Caesar and Woody was brought around by Milt Kamen, who also wrote for Caesar and thought Woody should, too. Kamen brought Woody into the room where Gelbart and Caesar were working on a script.

"I've got the young Larry Gelbart with me," Kamen announced.

"The young Larry Gelbart is *here*," Gelbart said, pointing to himself, and he and Caesar went back to work.

Woody sat down and listened for a while, then made a suggestion about a movie satire sketch. After about fifteen minutes, Caesar said, "Well, it's five o'clock, we might as well get started tomorrow. And you," acknowledging Woody for the first time, "you're hired." Woody was delighted. "I didn't ask any questions about money or any-thing. I would have been willing to work for coolie wages."

Woody also admires Gelbart's fatalism. "Larry was driving with me through Central Park one day, and he said, 'Did you hear that So-and-So dropped dead in Hollywood? You know, someday they're going to say that about me— "Hey, did you hear that Larry Gelbart dropped dead to-day?"' I've never forgotten that. That kind of indiffer-ence. You thought about it for a second."

Woody and Larry worked on three specials together. Two were for Caesar, the other for Art Carney. The Car-ney show, written in 1960, was called "Hooray for Love," and one sketch in it was a parody of Ingmar Bergman's film *Wild Strawberries*.

"That, and a sketch about Greenwich Village, was cere-bral, somewhat cool, as opposed to bumping your head," Gelbart says. "That was Woody's influence. I knew of the movie and the Village—anybody that didn't wasn't alive. But I think he could identify with it a little more because that is where he was really going."

Art Carney, Tony Randall, and Janis Paige played the parts. Woody considers the sketch interesting and amus-ing for something that was done fifteen years ago.

DISSOLVE TO ART CARDS:
1. *The Iceman Loveth*   (theater tickets)
2. *Raid on Love Nest at U.N.*   (headline tabloid)
3. *Desire Under the Chuck Wagon*   (movie sign)
4. *Bigamist Shot Twice*   (New York Times *article*)

188

5. *I'm Married on the Outside,*
   Crying on the Inside   (sheet music)
6. *Artie Shaw Marries*
   Lana Turner
7. *Mickey Rooney Marries*
   Ava Gardner
8. *Lana Turner Marries*
   Lex Barker
9. *Joe DiMaggio Marries*
   Marilyn Monroe
10. *Lex Barker Marries*
    Arlene Dahl   *(banner*
11. *Marilyn Monroe Marries*   *headlines)*
    Arthur Miller
12. *Arlene Dahl Marries*
    Fernando Lamas
13. *Frank Sinatra Marries*
    Ava Gardner
14. *Ava Gardner Marries*
    Artie Shaw
15. *Blind Date Runs Amuck,*
    Kills 12
16. *Love at the Top*
    of the Stairs   (theater program)
17. *Wild Strawberries*   (movie poster)

Orchestra hits movie opening music
Super titles
Telop #1 reads: "Svenska Pictures Present"
Telop #2: "An Ingmar Birdman Film"
Telop #3: "Strange Strawberries"
Telop #4: "Starring Björn Björnssen"
Telop #5: "Björd Björle"
Telop #6: "and Btöny Bcürtis"

Telop #7: "Written, directed, produced, and understood only by Ingmar Birdman"

Dissolve to Carney, old man sitting on bench. Beside the bench on a pole is a large clock with large numerals and no hands. He speaks to camera.

CARNEY

Le rok roka slat jamna snigel svenska.

Subtitle is superimposed: "I am Swedish."

Snara rycka till sig nysa vadra.

Subtitle reads: "I am 98 years old."

Mjuk jord soldat enda ensam losa nagon.

Subtitle reads: "Today I became a father."

Lugna snart tidigt sang ibland nagon nagra.

Subtitle reads: "How 'bout them egg rolls?"

Ute *forfallen* valta ogra *farbunjita.*

Subtitle reads: "Last night I had a dream."

Mask herre lara sig para sak madrass mogna kanske lara. Mota smalta medel inre bebo. Fraga golv kott fly smida. Dum utropa bors. Dyr gladja klen trotsa birst jup dasc tafatt yexa.

During above speech we see following subtitles in succession: "of when I was young" "and lived with my family."

Dissolve to Swedish home, 19th century. Carney, as young man, sits on stool at high desk. He has thin Bergman beard, wears jeweler's loupe in his eye as he works at something we do not see for a moment. As he works, knife in hand, Carney's voice is heard over.

190

CARNEY

En stund tilag svara riklig nagon lara.
Korg foda.

Subtitle reads: "I worked hard at my trade."

Ge sig upge formoda trask svan sopa.

"I cut holes in cheese."

Carney picks up what he is working on. It is a slice of cheese. As he meticulously finishes off a hole, Carney's voice continues:

Skatt lara gara om storm talt prov.

Subtitle reads: "I got 2 cents a hole."

Carney puts cheese slice on spindle, starts work on another.

Smaka kran hog. Bord sopa term.

Subtitle: "I was saving up for a nose job."

Okand tills pa stad.

Subtitle: "Cheese had driven my nose crazy."

Carney does nose business. He continues:

CARNEY

Olika vas flor.

Subtitle: "But I was happy."

Carney works happily.

Vaga my skst granskap undra stil.

Subtitle: "Until one day. . . ."

Door opens and Randall enters, calls to Carney. He wears identical beard.

RANDALL

Broder!

Subtitle: "Brother!"

Carney rises, embraces Randall.

191

CARNEY

Broder!

Subtitle: "Brother!"

RANDALL

(*pointing to door*) Slo rodna krop yenta!

Subtitle: "Meet my fiancee."

He extends his hand, a lovely obviously experienced, pig-tailed Paige enters.

CARNEY

Gren studsa krop oo-scoobie-doo!

As Randall speaks following, Paige stares at Carney with an unmistakable gleam in her eye.

RANDALL

Rodna brade tak fira stol.

Subtitle: "She works in a library."

Carney looks girl over, turns to camera.

CARNEY

Prata lura kemi spalt.

Subtitle: "Must be a circulating library."

Carney winks, nods at camera, turns back to Paige.

RANDALL

Fol kamp prosta.

Subtitle: "I'll be back."

Randall looks at Paige, then at Carney.

Latt blixt tycka om litvak.

Subtitle: "Stick to your cheese."

Hyra resa laglig.

Subtitle: "Or I'll *fix* your nose."

192

Carney and Randall laugh with accents. Randall kisses Paige on cheek, exits. Carney smiles weakly at Paige and self-consciously returns to his stool. Carney's voice is heard over as Paige smiles knowingly at Carney, takes a seat and begins powdering her nose.

CARNEY
Lag bly resa mindre stiga blot jord.
Kliva snora sum solg tunnelbana.

During the above, subtitle reads: "I went back to work." Next subtitle: "But my heart wasn't in my cheese." Paige slyly hikes bottom of her skirt so that her ankle is revealed. Carney looks away, then looks back at her. This time he wears two loupes in his eyes and uses them as binoculars. Paige looks up at him and smiles fetchingly. Embarrassed, Carney removes loupes and quickly goes back to working on cheese. Paige stands, and with her back to Carney, begins to straighten her stocking seams. Carney lifts a piece of cheese and surreptitiously peeks at her action through a hole in the cheese.

CARNEY
Gaster kupe klaga.

Subtitle: "Don't walk on me."

CARNEY
Forlora lasa karlek.

Subtitle: "I was in love."

Bo los broder.

Subtitle: "But she was my brother's."

Lokal finna plats.

Subtitle: "And we had an understanding."

193

Mogna kan mig amna.

Subtitle: "I didn't touch his girls."

Harre sak mogna.

Subtitle: "And he didn't wear my sport jackets."

Carney is carving at the cheese with one eye on Paige.
Carney's voice continues with simultaneous subtitles.

Gaba kort brev.

Subtitles: "It was very hard to work."

Carney holds up piece of cheese and instead of holes, he
has carved a large heart. He puts piece of cheese down,
lifts heart-shaped cut-out and puts it in his mouth and
chews. Old man's voice is heard, followed by subtitle.

Skota befla okide.

Subtitle: "I was eating my heart out."

Carney resumes work, pretends not to notice that Paige is
playfully tiptoeing up behind him. She plays with a
strand of his hair, he shakes her off, works. She tickles his
ear, he shakes his head again.

He bites his lower lip, fighting temptation. With a laugh,
Paige pulls loupe from his eye and runs across room. He
protests as he gets off stool, goes to her.

CARNEY

Forbinda!

PAIGE
(holding loupe behind her back)
Neg, neg, neg!

CARNEY

Ya, ya, ya!

Standing in front of her, he puts his arms around her to
get the loupe. She kisses him full on the lips. He reacts in
horror. She slaps his face.

194

PAIGE

Bolag avsluta!

Subtitle: "How dare you!"

Kula byra buss vid!

Subtitle: "I'm a librarian!"

CARNEY

Jaga kyska. . . . (*more Swedish*)

Pantomimes the kiss, then tenderly:

Ingrid Bergman. Jaga kronika. . . .

Pantomimes sock on the jaw, then:

Ingemar Johannsen!

Starts to walk away. She laughs gaily, grabs him, kisses him again. As they hold kiss, door opens and Randall re-enters.

RANDALL

Ooooooh—

Sees them kissing. Carney looks up at Randall.

CARNEY

Lara rada soffa gherkin.

Subtitle: "I'm in a pickle."

RANDALL

Eva—yenta—tugabar. Rakna vagga ring-a-ding?

CARNEY

Ring-a-ding.

PAIGE

Uppge stanna duglig. . . .

Subtitle: "The minute you left . . ."

PAIGE

(*cont'd.*) Hopa vark syra lugna.

195

She points at Carney.
Subtitle: "He came on like gangbusters!"
Randall grabs Carney by the collar, shakes him, angrily.

RANDALL
Avtal fria! Fria!

CARNEY
(protesting) Neg! Neg! Neg!

RANDALL
Slag punktlig broder!
Subtitle: "You are no longer my brother!"

Ren broder bevis broder!
Subtitle: "The most we can be is half-brothers!"
He rips one half of Carney's beard off with appropriate sound effect and then rips half of his own beard off with same sound effect. He hustles to the door, stopping at the desk.

Hoga mogen ratt fink!
He gives Carney a big piece of cheese.
Subtitle: "Don't forget your cheese."
He pushes Carney to door, goes back to desk.

RANDALL
(cont'd.) Flod strova cooga mooga!
Subtitle: "And take your holes, too!"
He picks up pieces of cheese, hurls them at a despondent Carney, who stands in doorway watching as Randall goes back to Paige, puts his arms around her comfortingly.

RANDALL
(cont'd.) Eva . . . Eva. . . .
They kiss violently. She looks at Carney at door, laughs mockingly.

196

Dissolve to Carney, as old man on bench. As he talks subtitles appear simultaneously.

CARNEY

Vara svar orolig retrar. . . .

Subtitle: "That happened 80 years ago."

Ros rutna doft.

Subtitle: "I've been sitting here ever since."

Rund rinna trygg.

Subtitle: "And my dream has a moral."

CARNEY

(cont'd.) Skola safir rutt.

Subtitle: "Love is like cheese."

Dela skarp . . .

Subtitle: "What undoes a mouse . . ."

Dela gripa . . .

Subtitle: "Undoes a man."

He gets up, starts to walk off, stops, then to camera:

La-la-la-la-la sla hav, skarp!

Waves slowly
Subtitle: "Th-th-th-that's all, folks!"
Music hits: Porky Pig closing theme
Iris to black
Dissolve super of "The Bjend" and Wild Strawberries *card*

The Bergman parody was the last writing Woody did for television for several years because he began performing as a stand-up and then became involved in films.

In 1968 and 1970 he had television specials of his own,

197

which he wrote. One, with Billy Graham, Candice Bergen and the Fifth Dimension, was part of the Kraft series of specials and came about only because a scheduled show with songwriter Jimmy Webb had fallen through. Woody's show did not get a high rating. The other was with Liza Minnelli and that one too, by TV standards anyway, did not draw a gigantic audience.

Woody is not keen on working in television. One problem is that sponsors have control over what is aired. Larry Gelbart once described working with sponsors this way: "We did a little thing on the 'Chevy Show' about a Dick Clark-type of band show with dancing, and there were lines like, 'Thanks for coming here instead of doing your homework,' and 'Here's a record I get an awful lot of money for playing.' Art Carney played the disc jockey and it was hilarious. But the sponsors came in with cross faces and said, 'We can't offend teenagers,' because, I don't know, they steal a lot of Chevys, I guess. They just went page by page and said, 'This is controversial and this is wrong and this is too strong.'"

Also, TV programs fight for quantitative ratings. "It's not like a movie, where if it is a great film like *Paths of Glory* but no one goes to see it it still eventually becomes amortized and also passes into the literature of film," Woody says. "TV is a one-shot deal. It's also a small screen, so it's harder to be really effective."

But perhaps most important is that Woody's primary medium is film, where he has both artistic control and permanence. "Somebody who is terrific on radio or television is like a Renaissance painter who worked on sand. You have to pick a medium that has some staying power. Stage is fun but if you're trying to accumulate a body of

198

work with substance to it, you need film. It has a chance to grow with time. And TV has a tendency to hurt your drawing power in films. Exposure makes you kind of familiar. If they can see one of my movies every year or year and a half, that's nice. They make a commitment to come and see you. On TV you're in the house for free and they can switch the dials back and forth."

He also avoids talk shows. "The problem with those talk shows is that I'm expected to be funny for an hour and and a half. It's a big strain. You're at peak tension because you can't let an opportunity go by without scoring. That's what they want of you. But it's easier than coming out for ten or fifteen minutes, because it's so short a time and you may not register. On the rare occasions I do go on talk shows—and I haven't done one since *Sam* came out—I only go on for the whole thing. An hour and a half is worthwhile. There are several million people watching. It's a nice score."

That's now. Early in his career Woody went on all the shows he could. The first show he was on was "P.M. East" with Mike Wallace, and Woody appeared on it a half-dozen times. "When I went on the Wallace show, it was a lark. I didn't think I'd be a comic. You know, two weeks and I'd be back writing. The first time I was on I prepared a monologue and ad libbed an interview. They called a couple of days later to say they had received a lot of phone calls and letters, so I went back. One time I woke up and realized I was on the show that night, so I went to F.A.O. Schwarz and bought a hammer and peg set. I got on and said, 'I'm going off comedy, I'm doing social commentary with a peg set. When the British took over Suez I had this to say,' and I hammered some pegs. I just didn't care. He

199

had me on with Barbra Streisand and the two of us were just great together. We were just a couple of schnooks when we went there. I didn't do the Johnny Carson show until years later. As I began to get more successful, I began to take things more seriously."

Woody likes Carson. "He was great when I was on his show. If I said I needed a line worded just this way, it would be there. He scores himself but he gets a kick out of it when you score. He is one of the really good, really witty MCs around. He really makes me laugh. They don't have a comparable person to him in the film business."

For a few years, Woody was occasionally the substitute host when Carson was on vacation, and he liked the work. "Hosting is completely different from coming on as a guest. It's tough to come on for twenty minutes and explode it. But as a host you're there for an hour and a half and you can ask questions of the guest, the camera is on the guest and you're not under the gun. You score when you can. There's just nothing to it in terms of technique, but Carson is fabulous." Because of his admiration for Carson, Woody made one of his few appearances at a dinner in his honor at the Americana Hotel in New York some years ago. Several big comics were there—Buddy Hackett, Joey Bishop, Phil Foster. Woody was the first or second speaker and perhaps the only one to prepare new material for the event, like: "You know, Johnny just got married. I've known him for years. We're old friends. I knew him before he was married when he was still dating Mahalia Jackson." After he finished, Woody made like he was going to the men's room and instead left the hotel: "I don't like those kind of events."

Despite his ambivalent feelings about working in television, in December 1971 Woody wrote, directed, and starred in a political satire special for the Public Broadcasting Service (PBS) that was to have been aired in February 1972. It was originally titled "The Woody Allen Comedy Special" but later was changed to "The Politics of Woody Allen." It was never shown.

Woody's fee for acting in the special was $135, the minimum scale. He donated his services as writer and director because, as he said at the time, "I like public television and I want to support it. The commercial networks offer you no freedom at all." PBS offered freedom but ultimately withdrew it.

Privately, PBS felt the show was potentially too offensive to the Nixon Administration. Publicly, they said that the portrayal of presidential candidates (Nixon, Hubert Humphrey, and George Wallace) would mean that equal time would have to be granted if they asked for it. The show was replaced by one featuring comedian Pat Paulsen, a bona fide candidate for president in the New Hampshire primary. No one asked for equal time.

Woody's intention was to make a "little funny documentary" satirizing the Nixon Administration. He tried "to find a character in the administration that would give me a chance to satirize all its branches, and I thought somebody like Henry Kissinger would be perfect." Henry Kissinger became Harvey Wallinger, and Woody played him.

In the publicity that followed the show's cancellation, Woody was widely quoted as having said in it that he "loathed President Nixon." What he actually said was that he loathed the Nixon Administration, but he added that had John Kennedy or Lyndon Johnson been in power, the show would have satirized *them.*

"The Harvey Wallinger Story" was both broad and innocuous. What follows is exerpted from both Woody's script and the final film version.

A narrator begins as newsreel footage of various 1968 scenes appears: "Nineteen sixty-eight, an election year, and the United States is swept by turmoil at home and abroad. Men vie for the Presidency, the highest elected office in the world with the exception of Pope, although the President does not get to wear a red suit. . . . The Democratic party turns to Hubert Humphrey, a man of style and grace [Humphrey, dressed in academic robes, stumbles]. While Humphrey publicly sides with the Johnson war policies, in private he has his own opinion. [Probably making the second part of a point, Humphrey instead appears to be making a universally used finger gesture for indicating displeasure.]

"The Republicans choose a man of force and magnitude —of personal charisma and a profound grasp of major issues—but that man refuses the nomination and they settle for Richard Nixon.

"The new President carefully chooses the men who will surround him. His Vice-President is a man whose personal magnetism and charisma equal the President's. His Secretary of Defense is Melvin Laird, who has a plan to end the Vietnamese War, so complicated that only two people in the world understand it and neither of them is Laird. Promising the country law and order, Nixon appoints his former law partner John Mitchell as Attorney General.

Mitchell has many ideas for strengthening the country's law-enforcement methods and is hampered only by lack of funds and the Constitution. . . . He invites into his inner circle of decision-making—and relies heavily on the advice of—his old friend Harvey Wallinger. Indeed, not a single action, neither foreign nor domestic, is taken without the advice of Wallinger, and many acknowledge that he, more than anyone in the Cabinet, is the second most powerful man in the country."

"It's not just a work relationship," says a White House aide in an interview. "It's a personal relationship as well. Harvey is one of the only people who can make the President laugh. He comes up behind him and tickles him."

"Nobody goes in to see the President without going through Harvey Wallinger," says a politician. "If you want something done, you've got to be in good with Harvey. If Mrs. Nixon wants to kiss her husband, she has to kiss Harvey first."

A crony of the President explains how Wallinger and Nixon became friends: "Mr. Nixon needed someone to go for coffee and bring up hamburgers and general errands. He didn't want merely an errand boy, but a young lawyer with promise."

"I didn't think it would work out at first," Wallinger says, "because Mr. Nixon sent me for a dozen roast beefs on rye and five regular coffees and somehow I got it wrong and brought back a bacon and tomato on toast. . . . Now you don't do that to a man like Mr. Nixon. . . . He immediately suspected a Communist plot, but I soon managed to convince him. . . ."

Wallinger speaks on a variety of important issues— among them segregation and Nixon's Checkers Speech.

"Many years ago, there was slavery in this country. Mr. Nixon has always regretted that. I've seen him weep over stories of how families were broken up and sold—one to pick cotton, one to a cruel master. . . . Mr. Nixon has always been outspoken in his views on the issues that divide America.

"I helped Dick Nixon write his Checkers Speech. . . . He was in trouble, no question about it. . . . Eisenhower was campaigning against alleged corruption in the Truman Administration and here Dick was accused of accepting large outside donations to his campaign fund and we sat around. . . . I tried to come up with some image the American public would buy to show he was—you know—a good scout. . . . I suggested Pat sit next to him. . . . I thought it would be nice if the camera could pan over her —if you remember, it did. . . . I wanted her to be holding a little prayer shawl." And whose idea was Checkers? "Both mine and Mr. Nixon's. . . . We needed some symbol to wipe out any notion the public might have that wasn't one hundred percent wholesome. . . . He wanted to have a Miss America contest going on in the background. . . . He also thought perhaps if he were dressed in an Uncle Sam suit . . . red, white, and blue . . . with the beard . . . a rented beard. . . . Then I hit on the idea of telling America he owned a dog—a spaniel. . . . You know, Americans can never really dislike anyone who owns a dog. . . . At first he didn't want to—he thought if maybe he came out dressed like a little boy with Dwight Eisenhower holding his hand—they could perhaps do an endearing little thing but—er. . . . I persuaded him that all he really needed was to talk about Checkers."

"Who is Harvey Wallinger?" the narrator asks. "What

204

is the secret of the man behind the President? Where did he come from and how is it that he exerts such a hold over the decisions that affect us all?

"His father, Dr. Herbert Wallinger, makes a good living performing open-heart surgery by mail. His mother, the former Anna Cheswick, is a newspaper woman who had an affair with Mussolini until she discovered he was Italian. . . . At Harvard University he is a political science major. His heroes are Aaron Burr and the Kaiser."

The Eisenhower years are described as "a time of peace and contentment for America and the Republican Party. Harvey Wallinger surprises intimates by getting married to Renata Baldwin, daughter of a newspaper magnate and gym major at Vassar College. Vice-President Nixon says a few warm words at the reception [Woody and Diane Keaton as Renata are shown asleep at the head table. Interspersed with shots of them is newsreel footage of Nixon extolling the wonders of corn blight control].

"They honeymoon on the Rockefeller farm in Venezuela, which Harvey remembers fondly: 'Rockefeller's farm was bigger than Venezuela itself. Not many people understand this concept, but the entire nation is a possession of the Rockefeller family. . . . He hires the citizens to walk around and act like citizens—but he could close the country anytime he wants.' "

Later, "he and his wife divorce. She claims he is a registered Republican and charges him with having committed adultery with a member of the Democratic party."

"I would not have minded if he had committed adultery with a member of his own party," Renata says, "but I felt that cheating with a Democrat was immoral."

"Sex is a capricious thing," Wallinger says. "Sometimes

205

I feel like making love to a Republican. Generally I like to wait and see what the Russians do first."

Divorced, Wallinger is frequently seen "escorting some of the capital's most exciting women." One of them is a nun, Sister Mary Elizabeth Smith, who says: "He's an unbelievable swinger, a freak."

"My social life has been greatly exaggerated," Wallinger says. "I like pretty women—who doesn't? I like sex, but not un-American sex." What distinguishes American sex? "If you're ashamed of it. I think sex without guilt, without shame, it's not good; it becomes almost pleasurable."

The show concluded with the narrator saying: "Harvey Wallinger continues to do his job. Some may criticize him, others may praise him, but everyone—will forget him."

Had Woody agreed to cut the scenes of Sister Mary Elizabeth Smith, Humphrey's hand gesture, and one where Wallinger discloses that, "Dick is out of the country a lot and sometimes Pat calls up and asks me to come over, but I say, 'no,' " the show would probably have been aired. But he thought the scenes should stay in.

"It was an honest disagreement," he said during the controversy over the show's cancellation. "They honestly felt the material should be cut and I honestly felt that it shouldn't. Everybody that saw it thought it was in enormously bad taste. It was in bad taste, there was no question about it. Because I'm a master of bad taste and it's hard to do anything about the administration that wouldn't be in bad taste. And so they decided not to air it because they felt that if the United States saw the show it would impair the morals of the country and turn the general population into a violent people. I thought it was

206

an innocuous but insulting show. It lacked maybe great political depth or insight, but it was a funny half hour. Those people who are against the administration would have loved it, and those who were for the administration would have written me off as a crackpot. It was all so silly. It wasn't Jonathan Swift. If the show had gone on as scheduled, it would have passed unnoticed."

Which is why Woody makes films.

11.
"It's not that I'm afraid to die, I just don't want to be there when it happens."

When Woody Allen was writing fifty jokes a day for celebrity clients of a public relations firm, he thought he was "in the heart of show business," so when he moved up to writing for television, he must have thought he was in its soul. Being a teen-ager and making thousands of dollars writing for big names and shows can have a limiting effect on one's aspirations. That was the case with Woody, until one day Abe Burrows asked him, "You don't want to be a television writer all your life, do you?"

"I wondered what he meant by that. I wondered, 'What's bad about writing for TV?' I thought it was wonderful to be a TV writer and never had any interest in writing for the theater. I never even went to a play until my late teens, although by accident I read *You Can't Take It with You* when I was in about the fourth grade. When I started going to the theater, I went to see all the come-

208

dies and most of the other plays. I was responsive to the comedies I saw, like *Born Yesterday* and *Teahouse of the August Moon.*"

Besides films, where Woody's knowledge is immense, he has watched and thought about stage comedy and drama carefully.

"When I get an idea for a play, I think to myself, 'What play does this most closely resemble that was successful?' *Don't Drink the Water* is based on the premise of a whole family living together and getting on each other's nerves, like Kaufman's *You Can't Take It with You.* The play is based on that source of comedy and on the structure of *Teahouse of the August Moon.* Nobody has pointed out the similarity, but it's true. *Play It Again, Sam* is modeled on *The Seven Year Itch.* I try to use the same tricks in structure because the subject matter and characters are different. In *The Seven Year Itch* a guy wakes up with another woman and is absolutely guilt-stricken and convinced that she is going to break up his marriage or a blackmailer is going to tell his wife. And I just reversed it. There is an enormous amount of similarity between the two plays, yet if you look at them, you couldn't mistake one for the other."

Although Woody changed as early as 1957 from being merely a television writer to being a television writer who aspired to writing for Broadway, his first play was not produced until 1966. Concentrating on becoming a stand-up comic intervened in the interim and then *What's New, Pussycat?* came along. So for a long time his closest association to writing for Broadway was walking in the theater district with Louise Lasser and telling her stories that began, "When I have my play produced. . . ."

209

His chance came when producer Max Gordon asked Woody to write a play. Gordon had become a fan of Woody's nightclub act and Woody was enchanted with Gordon because he had produced some of George S. Kaufman's plays and because "he could tell the difference between a good and a bad joke."

Woody wrote the play but Gordon did not like it, so Woody took *Don't Drink the Water* to another fan, David Merrick, who agreed to produce it. Woody decided to keep as director Bob Sinclair, who was left over from the deal with Gordon. Sinclair had not directed a play for perhaps thirty years but his credits included such hits as *The Women, Pride and Prejudice,* and *Dodsworth.* Since Woody had had several talks with him about the play, he felt obliged to keep him. "He was allegedly a protégé of George S. Kaufman," Woody says, "but that was loose talk." Lou Jacobi was signed for the male lead.

While the play did very well once it got to Broadway, getting it there is one of the great show business horror stories.

It began when Woody was in England filming his small part in *Casino Royale,* an extravagant picture which kept him in London for six months for a total of about a week's work. The rest of the time he spent working on the play, going to museums, and playing high-stakes poker.

A cable came from Merrick saying he wanted Vivian Vance to play the female lead, even though Woody had written the part "with a more Jewish character in mind. They insisted she would be hilarious and she had name value and all of that. And I made a mistake by agreeing. Not that there's anything wrong with Vivian Vance—just that she was the wrong person for the character. It was a cheesy attempt at commercialism rather than correct casting. It would have been just as wrong to cast Kim Stanley."

Vivian Vance was signed, however, and the play went into rehearsals. It opened for a tryout in Philadelphia to mixed notices but great laughs. But the play was a shambles. "The direction was the worst in the world," Woody says. "No one knew what to do. People were standing around. It was a non-directed play." It became officially non-directed when Sinclair was fired.

"The play was falling apart," Woody remembers. "We couldn't interest a director. Audiences were not coming. You couldn't get a seat to *Breakfast at Tiffany's* with Mary Tyler Moore, which was also playing in Philadelphia, but one Saturday matinee we had three, maybe six rows in the audience."

Woody kept to himself in his hotel room, rewriting. The cast, playing half a new show, half an old one, would get line changes at noon for a 1:00 P.M. performance; how they remembered them was "miraculous" to Woody.

The show was saved for the first time when Stanley Prager agreed to come on as director. He brought enthusiasm, confidence, and competence. Woody made more structural changes. The show was restaged. The play moved to Boston. Woody developed a high fever and "ran up an enormous bill at the Ritz for juices and stuff. Then I got the idea to make the priest the narrator. I kept rewriting and the show started to coagulate. But the laughs were always in it, even though there were weak spots and it was soft as a blob."

There were also soft spots in the cast. The part of the ambassador was changed several times; the ingenue four times. In all there were thirteen cast changes—probably a record for a non-musical play.

In addition, small disasters kept occurring. The night before opening in Boston, the wife of one of the leading actors died and the stage manager had to play the part. Dick Libertini, who played the priest/narrator, collapsed on another night and couldn't go on. "It was just a madhouse," Woody says. "But through it all Tony Roberts remained cheerful, strong, steady and got his lines [Roberts, who was in the stage and screen versions of *Play It Again, Sam,* has become one of Woody's closest friends]. And Lou held up very well. Lou's Lou. He's a funny machine."

What pulled the play together at last in Woody's opinion was replacing Vivian Vance with Kay Medford. "Suddenly she became a hilarious character. Then we came to New York and played previews and I constantly rewrote until two or three days before it opened. Then we froze it."

Don't Drink the Water was lucky to get to Broadway when it did. At one point Merrick considered closing it out of town and then opening it in Florida at a theater he had dealings with, hoping to get it back in shape for New York. "David thought the show was so funny and that we had just gotten a bad break by hiring the wrong director and maybe the wrong cast in certain parts. But a lot of hard work, and the addition of Stanley Prager was the key —suddenly a guy coming in with no reservations about the show saying, 'All right, everyone on your feet, we're going to rehearse this thing and we really want to work hard and give the material a fair test, now let's get a little movement going here.' On that rise that he started I

212

made important structural changes and it reached its apogee with the addition of Kay Medford. Lou got every laugh; there wasn't a laugh in there he didn't get. And he got twenty enormous laughs that weren't written, just from his body movements.

"David Merrick behaved great through the whole thing with one or two exceptions. He was a terrific producer to have around in many ways. He got me what I wanted when I wanted it. But he was not encouraging. He was like the angel of death. He'd come to the show and say, 'Oh, they're going to back the scenery truck up to the theater Monday.' He came to Boston once and saw the show and walked out, and I called New York and said, 'How can you do that? These people have worked so hard.' In New York we had an argument about a line that he didn't want put in the show. He was right, as it turned out." (The most celebrated confrontation between Woody and Merrick was in Washington, D.C., when *Sam* was trying out there. Merrick, dapperly dressed in a blue suit, suggested to Woody, who was considerably less dapper, that he change a line. "David," Woody said, "I've made over a million dollars in my life by not listening to men in blue suits.")

On opening night Woody went with Mickey Rose to the theater and looked at it, then they went to the Automat and had dinner. After that they went and shot some pool at McGirr's Billiard Academy. There was a party at Jack Rollins' house following the show which they went to and sat around waiting for the reviews—the only time he has ever done that. In contrast, the night *Play It Again, Sam* opened, he went to Dinty Moore's for dinner with a few friends, stayed with Louise Lasser (they were separated but still friendly), and on the way home in the morning was stopped by a lady he had never met who congratulated him on the good notices—the first report of them he had.

The reviews of *Don't Drink the Water* were mixed—somewhere between great and terrible. But they were the kind of reviews that had people buying tickets the next day and for a year and a half after that. Had the show not been forced to move twice to other theaters, it would have played longer.

"The laughs were enormous," Woody says of the play. "I tell you, they were *enormous*. I can't tell you the amount of laughter in that show because that is what it was about. I wrote it for laughs—I didn't know how to survive any other way, and Lou Jacobi and Kay Medford were hysterically funny. It was reminiscent of the Kaufman things without the finesse. Stagehands said they never heard so many laughs. It was so farcical and silly, and Lou is such a favorite of those audiences from Great Neck. It played like a house afire. It played well on opening night, but the criticism is true—it did have all those structural flaws and it was that thin. I never for a second doubted that it would be a hit, though. There was no question in my mind that audiences were going to respond to it. But it was a true nightmare. I remember David Merrick saying to me in Philadelphia, "Well, you're up to your ass in show business."

In *Play It Again, Sam* Woody wanted to write not only a funny play, but a vehicle for him to act in as well. The play was written at the time his marriage to Louise Lasser was breaking up; by the time it went into rehearsal she had just about moved out of the house. While the story did not actually occur in real life, "What did occur is that married friends would say, 'Oh, we know a nice girl for you.' They'd introduce me to a girl and it would be an awkward evening because those things are always awkward, and I'd make a fool of myself frequently. Then I would find that the wives of my friends, who I wouldn't in a million years think of as being lovers with, I'd be natural around them and real. And that's what gave me the idea. You're pressing with a stranger and you're totally at home with friends because you don't give a damn, and she's the one who sees you as a real person, whereas the other people see you as a nervous kind of person or a grotesque or something."

So he tried to write *Sam* for himself. Which meant that he would not be required to act, because while Woody is fine within a certain range of character, he is not, nor has he any pretensions of being, an actor. "I play me. I couldn't play Romeo or the part of Michael Corleone in *The Godfather.* As long as the range is limited to a certain number of things, I can do that. It's like Hope working with Crosby—Hope gives the correct response; it's not acting in the sense that Marlon Brando acts. I can do that well myself as long as it's the half-dozen emotions that I'm familiar with and can play. I can act realistically within a certain narrow range."

The narrow range for *Sam* required Woody to play a man being divorced by his wife who tries so hard to succeed with other women that he fails to be himself. But only Woody of all those connected with *Sam* has such a limited view of his acting capabilities in the show. David

215

Merrick, who produced it, Joseph Hardy, who directed it, Tony Roberts, who acted in it, all claim that Woody grew into the part.

"When he started he was playing himself embarrassed," Hardy says. "He was reading his own lines and I don't think he liked the way they sounded when he read them. 'If I were the actor up there and I were the author out here,' he said to me, 'I'd come up behind you and say, "What do you have that clown in this play for? Get him out. He's ruining my work."' Which wasn't true. I think about the second week of rehearsal Woody started to like it a lot and we were all having fun. He liked the acting of other people that he could bounce off of. What I really had to do was get him to be enlarged as an entity onstage. He progressed through various stages of acting, and retrogressed as the play went on. He could cut ten minutes off the play by streaking through it if he wanted to get out early, even though he always protected the laughs."

"I think Merrick and Hardy were being kind of romantic when they said how much I developed as an actor in *Sam,*" Woody argues. "The truth of the matter is, I wrote that for myself, I remember being in a hotel room in Chicago and in my house when I was writing it, saying the lines out loud so that I could do it in my sleep. A real actor shows up and gets a part written by a playwright and then thinks about it and adds little shadings to it and gives him mannerisms and a rounded and developed character. And when you see that done to perfection, like with the Lunts, it's miraculous. I'm not like that. I am that character. I wrote it for me as natural as could be. My room for improvement was twenty percent—getting over ner-

216

vousness, getting the words down pat, getting a little familiarity with the stuff."

One thing Woody did learn from *Sam* is the difference between acting in films and on stage. "Onstage, you get to know the place so well that you can think about anything when you perform. I've been onstage in the midst of scenes getting big laughs and thinking as I was saying it, 'Hey, this is a pretty well-written scene, I think I constructed this well, but that I should have done. . . .' And actors are forever telling stories about how Gielgud and people like that will be moving the audience beyond belief and thinking, 'Gee, I sent my laundry out with four pairs of shorts this morning and they only sent back three, or did I. . . .' And it's true. When you're doing a play you find you can keep your mind on the play easily and your thoughts wander. With a film, you do such short bursts of scenes. To me it's such a pain in the neck to have to act in a movie. I enjoy setting the thing up, then I have to put on my costume and the collar itches, and then I have to get in front of the camera and dredge up the energy to act startled when she pulls out a knife. It's such an effort. But one reason I can switch on and off is that it's like playing poker for money or not for money. When I'm playing for money, or if I'm at a party and I want to impress someone—generally a woman—there's a switch that goes on. What helps me turn on immediately on the set is that I wrote the material and have more understanding of it than most actors. I'm writing to accommodate already existing feelings. I try not to write something I can't do. I like to work with Diane and Louise because I have so much confidence in them that I worry about myself. I don't even think about them. They're so accomplished in my eyes that all I think about is myself and is the camera getting it, or have we moved too far to the right?"

What Woody can do onstage that he can't do in front of a camera is fool around. "If Woody blows a line, he just goes up," Diane Keaton says, who played in both the stage and screen versions of *Sam* as well as *Sleeper* and *Love and Death*. "He can't continue the scene. Tony [Roberts] and I can mess up a line and go on, but not Woody. And then you start laughing. We'd just actually start laughing and couldn't stop. I mean the discipline some nights was really bad. And then a couple of nights Woody would do Groucho onstage and Tony would do Sidney Greenstreet, in front of all those people. They'd agree to do it beforehand. Tony once had his pants off when Woody came out for a glass of water and Woody came back on and couldn't talk, he was laughing so hard."

While *Play It Again, Sam* received fine reviews and lots of laughter, it has never really been given credit for the innovation and theatricality Woody, Hardy, and set designer William Rittman came up with.

"The thing I loved about the play was the apparitions," Hardy says. "They were pure theatricality. The film can't do that really. The theatrical concept of that is superb. They can just appear. Put spots directly overhead with three lighting levels. Walls had spaces that you couldn't see from the front and all those hot lights were there. If he was talking stage left, she could appear stage right center. Characters could turn and walk into the wall. It's not cinematic. I've not known of a modern comedy where this happened. As they talked about the girl slamming the

218

door in his face, for instance, as he talked she would just appear; it was just up in his study and she came out of the wall and they walked over to a door. Or when he talked about rowboating in Central Park, a rosewood and leather chair and footstool suddenly became a boat.

"The play was as good and in some aspects better in London. Dudley Moore was a more accomplished actor than Woody, so in certain aspects Woody would never give himself entirely to a certain situation. For instance, when Woody and the girl spent the night together, Woody would always go for the comedic aspects alone. Dudley did invest it with a certain vulnerability, which Woody had trouble doing, because Woody's so bright and cerebral."

Woody intends to write serious plays for Broadway, which he may direct, perhaps, but not act in. His three one-act plays entitled *Sex, Death,* and *God*—the three things he thinks about the most—were to be staged during the 1973–74 season, but they required elaborate sets and it turned out producing them would cost $250,000— too great an initial cost to realistically expect ever making a profit. Had the plays been suitable for turning into a film, there would have been no trouble in putting them on Broadway and making the profit on the film sale. While still quite funny, the plays were nevertheless serious and constituted an important broadening of Woody's spectrum of writing. When he began writing he worshipped George S. Kaufman, but now he has passed beyond wanting to write solely for the laugh into a desire to write a good drama.

A play, of course, is much more a piece of writing than a film. "A play is fun to write," he says. "For three months you get up and just write. I'm much looser in a room by myself because I'm not in contact with the real world. It's when you go into rehearsal that the real world comes. You watch lines being done and realize that they are sentimental and mawkish and not funny. I have so little regard for film writing that I don't take it seriously enough to discipline myself. Now, a play is serious. I plan it out. I outline it. A movie script is just a shooting guide. A play is serious and I write it by myself, taking plenty of time and concentrating. For a movie, Mickey or Marshall come over and we pitch gags. The writing is just a suggestion. It tells me how many people and what props I need. I have to write a film on the set. When you decide where you're putting your camera on a shot, there's where you make it funny. When I'm sitting at home, I just can't know what it's going to be like.

"I would never write a play with someone. The fun of a play is writing it. You've got to wallow in it. Writing a play with someone else would be like calling in another director on a film.

"I like writing; I like playwriting; I like writing for *The New Yorker*. I like the pure joy of waking up in my house, having my breakfast, going into a room by myself, and writing. It's pleasurable because it's lazy and escapist. You don't have to deal with anybody, you don't have to see anybody, you're never on the line. There's nothing to the job—although I'm not saying writing comes easy."

Woody's humorous prose is the broadest of his writing, and in many ways it is the funniest. There are two kinds of humorous prose. One is stylish and filled more with chuckles than with laughs; the point is to tell an amusing and beguiling and perhaps informative story. The other sets out from the first word to make the reader laugh out loud, then doesn't let up; it is brittle, intellectual, and cosmopolitan, like S.J. Perelman's and Woody's. The first is crinkley-nosed; Perelman's and Woody's is punch-you-in-the-nose.

"I want people to read my stories without the slightest investment of intellect and laugh," Woody says. "I don't want them to have to read through two paragraphs of erudite references. I want them to start laughing almost immediately." (A typical beginning of an Allen story: "Of all the wonders of nature, a tree in summer is perhaps the most remarkable, with the possible exception of a moose singing 'Embraceable You' in spats.") While the stories do not require an intellectual commitment from the reader, they are nevertheless very intelligent and parody the widest spectrum of subjects, among them: ballet, pedantry, Ingmar Bergman films, death, organized crime, revolutionaries, psychiatrists, dieters, horror stories, detective stories, philosophy, college bulletins, *The Maltese Falcon*, practical essays, and the writing styles of Ernest Hemingway and Feodor Dostoevski.

In high school Woody was "a gigantic fan of Max Shulman's. *Gigantic.* To this day I can probably quote blocks of his writing. My friends and I were just insane about him. When I used to write my first abortive attempts at comedy, I would write in his style. Then the more I was introduced to Perelman and Robert Benchley, I got crazy about them. I think those two are the great comedy writers. I think the most you can say about many of the others is that some of them are sporadically funny. Perelman and Benchley have a much bigger armory of tricks. For instance, Sid Caesar had more tricks than Jackie Leonard, or Henny Youngman, who has a certain trick and he does it. Like a prizefighter who has a barrage of punches, such as Sugar Ray Robinson, Caesar had fifteen tricks. He could last an hour a week for ten years because he was coming at you from so many different directions. Benchley and Perelman are masters of all kinds of absurdities and non sequiturs. There's a certain funniness that Perelman and Benchley have, funny in a critical, hilarious way that Jonathan Winters is. They see life differently and have more funny ideas than Thurber or Lardner or any of those people."

Of all the writers of humorous prose, Perelman's style is by far the most distinctive and the most often imitated. His prose is dense—there are jokes on the way to jokes on the way to sentences on the way to paragraphs that are funny. He has made an art of names. In one sentence he can introduce "Gossip Gabrilowitsch, the Polish pianist; Downey Couch, the Irish tenor; Frank Falkovsky, the Jewish prowler; and myself, Clay Modeling." He has such an incredibly rococo and unique style—the names, sentence structure, esoteric, even exotic vocabulary, leads that have nothing to do with the story for the first three or four paragraphs and then come around to it—that is his and his alone.

"Perelman is so utterly unique and complex," Woody says. "You can't be influenced a little by him. You have to go so deeply that it shows all over the place. You can't write something that's a little Perelmanesque, just like you can't play a little bit like Errol Garner. There are so many points that are recognizable. It's interesting in a peripheral way that I'm trying to do names more like Benchley; they have a distinctive style and are hilarious but they are less descriptive than Perelman's." Woody uses European names—Fears Hoffnung, Horst Wasserman, and Gunther Eisenbud; Mafia names—Thomas (The Butcher) Covello, Albert (The Logical Positivist) Corillo, and Kid Lipsky; two chessplayers playing a game by mail named Gossage and Vardebedian; and a private eye named Kaiser Lupowitz, who could have been named by Perelman.

Virtually all of Woody's humorous essays appear in *The New Yorker*. As when he began performing and was unsure of audiences, he did not have great faith that the editors there would like his material. The first story he sent them was "The Gossage–Vardebedian Papers," a series of increasingly hostile letters between two men playing a game of chess by mail, each of whom is convinced that the other is deranged.

"I thought the first thing they bought from me was a freak," he recalls. "I thought, 'Well, I'm never going to sell them anything again in my life.' I remember they said they wondered if I was willing to rewrite the ending. And, you know, I would have been willing to turn the ending into an aquafoil. Then I sent them the next thing and they bought it right off and I started to feel more confident. Now I'm sending in stuff that is so broad. I've tried to write things for *The New Yorker* broader than they've published in years and years; I think I can write the broadest stuff for them of anybody. When I first wrote for them I always assumed that it had to be complex, because I'm probably their most illiterate writer—my grammar and spelling are just laughable. What I've been trying to do is get more and better laughs clearer and easier."

Woody refers to his work for *The New Yorker* as "sheer dessert." Not that he means to slight the magazine or the form his work takes—only that it is the easiest to do of all the things he does. The reason is simple—it is all concentrated on three or four pages. It is not a year's work involving a hundred people, like a film; nor is it a forty-five-minute monologue that takes a year to write and rewrite and perfect. It is just three or four pages of the funniest stuff he can come up with, and he enjoys the luxury of not having to filter it through a lot of other sensibilities and stages.

That he feels he is unable to write serious prose does not stop Woody from making serious points or dealing with serious issues, however big the laugh is around them. There are references to death, for example, in practically everything he writes.

—It is impossible to experience one's own death objectively and still carry a tune.

—Death is one of the few things that can be done as easily lying down.

—The thing to remember is that each time of life has its appropriate rewards, whereas when you're dead it's hard to find the light switch.

—I do not believe in an afterlife, although I am bringing a change of underwear.

—The chief problem about death, incidentally, is the fear that there may be no afterlife—a depressing thought, particularly for those who have bothered to shave.

—Dying doesn't make you thirsty. Unless you get stabbed after eating herring.

—Also, there is the fear that there is an afterlife but no one will know where it is being held.

—It's not that I'm afraid to die. I just don't want to be there when it happens.

—Death, incidentally, is one of the worst things that can happen to a Cosa Nostra member, and many prefer simply to pay a fine.

—Death is an acquired trait.

Death Knocks, which appeared in *The New Yorker,* is a parody of Bergman's film *The Seventh Seal.* In it, Nat Ackerman, a fifty-seven-year-old garment manufacturer, is called on one midnight by Death, who looks something like Nat. Death is new on the job and the two of them dicker over whether or not Nat will go right then. They agree to play gin rummy. If Nat wins, he gets an extra day; if he loses, they go right then. They also agree to play for a tenth of a cent a point. "I play better when money's at stake," Nat says. Nat wins. Death, grumbling that he didn't know that Nat was *really* playing for time, goes through his pockets and finds he doesn't have the money he owes:

DEATH
I have a few singles, not twenty-eight dollars.

NAT
All right, gimme what you got and we'll call it square.

225

DEATH

Listen, I need that money.

NAT

Why should you need money?

DEATH

What are you talking about? You're going to the beyond.

NAT

So?

DEATH

So—you know how far that is?

NAT

So?

DEATH

So where's gas? Where's tolls?

NAT

We're going by car!

DEATH

You'll find out. (*agitatedly*) Look—I'll be back tomorrow, and you'll give me a chance to win the money back. Otherwise I'm in definite trouble.

NAT

Anything you want. Double or nothing we'll play. I'm liable to win an extra week or a month. The way you play, maybe years.

DEATH

Meantime I'm stranded.

226

NAT

See you tomorrow.

In *Death*, the most Kafkaesque and serious of the three one-act plays, Kleinman, the main character, is trapped at the end by the maniac (Death) he and everyone else in the play has been frantically and bumblingly looking for. The maniac, who supposedly looks like each person he has killed, looks like Kleinman, who, just before he is stabbed, asks: "But why do you do it?"

"I'm a screwball. You think I know?"

"There *is* a preponderance of death jokes in what I write," Woody admits. "There are a lot of sex jokes, too. But I don't do them consciously. They just appear."

One reason the death jokes appear is that he is preoccupied with death. To him it is an irrational, hostile act on the part of the universe. He cites Tolstoy when he says that "any man over thirty-five with whom death is not the main consideration is a fool," and he adds that "the enemy is God and nature and the universe—that's what's killing us. The enemy is not the Chinese or the guy next door to you, the enemy is out there. That's what *Death* is all about, that guys are running around doing all that shit, fighting each other, making up all kinds of ways of dealing with stuff, and they don't know what they're doing."

This may be why, with his mind focused on such cosmic issues, he can reel off with ease such earthbound lines as, "It all began one day last January when I was standing in McGinnis' Bar on Broadway, engulfing a slab of the world's richest cheesecake and suffering the guilty, cholesterolish hallucination that I could hear my aorta congealing into a hockey puck." Or, "Her figure described a set of parabolas that could cause cardiac arrest in a yak."

So while Woody wishes that he could "write stuff that says something more," he is resigned, at least for now, to writing short pieces that go strictly for the laugh.

"I'm not trying to write stuff like Thurber or Ade wrote, that's kind of wry and clever and informative in certain ways. I'm going for the big laugh all the time. I want people to read it and laugh out loud. That to me is the most pleasurable thing. [He once said to his friend Tony Roberts, "I want them to laugh so hard they'll hate me."] When I come across a Benchley or Perelman essay that I haven't read before, it's a very enjoyable thing to read it."

Woody plans in the future to write at least one novel (*Getting Even* sold very well—about 30,000 hardcover copies and over 300,000 in paperback), because he thinks he could write a funny one and he feels there are so few. (The only funny novels he can think of are the Max Shulman novels, *Portnoy's Complaint, Catch-22* "and maybe" *Catcher in the Rye.*) But it will not be for a while: "I feel it is the kind of work one should do when he's not young and vigorous. I feel that the six months or a year that it would take to write a novel, I should be writing for the theater, directing movies, and starring in them and stuff, because I think there will be a time in my life when I won't want the strenuousness of those kinds of things. Also, one has to realize that there is generally less impact from novels than from films."

While there is no comparison between the amount of money a popular writer and a popular filmmaker can make—popular filmmakers make millions of dollars—money does not seem to be an issue with Woody. Al-

228

though he was once quoted as saying, jokingly, "Everything good I've ever written is the result of a sharp, searing blow. I smash my occipital area with a heavy mallet, then write down whatever comes. I do it for the money," money is not the overriding consideration with him since he is financially secure for life.

What are considerations for him are two things—that "I have some gift, however minimal, and I feel obliged to exercise it the best way I can," and that he will be remembered as one of the great American comedians. In order to be fairly remembered, appreciated, and judged over time, film allows him the widest latitude to exercise his talent. And so, while he is and always has been primarily a writer, as long as he remains vigorous he intends to spend the bulk of his time writing for film and the stage rather than for the printed page. There will, however, certainly be a regular flow of short essays filled with such illuminating social commentary as, "Other illicit activities engaged in by Cosa Nostra members included gambling, narcotics, prostitution, hijacking, loan-sharking, and the transportation of a large whitefish across the state line for immoral purposes."

12.
"People tell me
there are a lot of guys like me,
which doesn't explain why
I'm lonely."

"I once had an idea for a short story in which a guy was trying to put together the ultimate survival kit," Woody said one day during the filming of *Love and Death*. "There were collapsible fishing poles, and fish hooks, and lights, and pocket knives, and a compass, but he was never able to make it perfect. I think that's true."

If there is a word that sums up Woody Allen, it is survival. In his work, as with many comedians', his character is under constant threat but always manages to triumph over dire consequences and escape, if only into new threats. But temporarily, anyway, he survives. And since survival is ultimately impossible, Woody's fierce determination to achieve it in both artistic and personal terms makes him rather unsentimental but terribly romantic; an assessment he does not share completely.

"I think I am sentimental. I think I'm a sucker for cheap

sentimentality—as long as it's my own. I always hate the other guy's self-indulgence. As far as romantic, if you think being against the universe is a romantic position, then I agree. Take *Love and Death*. I guess you could say it's vaguely romantic in concept. But any existential obsession, even as frivolous as my film, carries with it romantic overtones automatically. Philosophical thought of men like, say, Russell and Dewey or even Hegel may be dazzling but it's sober and uncharismatic. Dostoevski, Camus, Kierkegaard, Berdyayev—the minds I like—I consider romantic. I guess I equate 'dread' with romance, which is why I'm not invited to more parties. The trick, as I see it, is to be Byronic without appearing Moronic. Malraux spoke about art being the last defense against death. That, to me, is romantic."

Time spent with Woody Allen is time spent with a man who is enormously intelligent, creative, witty, knowledgeable—and alienated. He deals with most people in a reserved and quiet way, never liking close contact. With the exception of a few friends, he communicates and deals with other people through his work; he would rather not encounter them personally. There is in him a basically controlled misanthropy but a basically uncontrolled aversion to things mechanical. He *does* break toasters. He takes out his anger on non-human things. Watching him butter a piece of bread is alarming; he attacks it with the knife.

"People tell me there are a lot of guys like me, which doesn't explain why I'm lonely," Mort Sahl once said, referring to his ability to make his audience feel they share his concerns, fears, and outrages. There are apparently millions of people who share Woody Allen's sensibilities, fears, failures—and also share his triumphs in spite of them that enable him to survive and prosper, if defensively, in the face of a philosophically and pragmatically impossible world. But that body of shared experience provides him no solace save the peripheral one of making his films successful, which allows him to work unimpeded by financial restrictions. He remains lonely, working hard at creative survival. A measure of immortality is achievable in films, and he appreciates that. It is, however, not enough.

"I don't want to achieve immortality through my work," he says. "I want to achieve it through not dying."

Acknowledgments

In a roundabout way, this book happened because Gerry Walker and the other editors of *The New York Times Magazine* commissioned me to write a piece on Woody Allen, which I did and, alas, turned in the day *Time* ran a cover story on him. Richard Kluger then suggested I turn misfortune into penury by doing a book for him on Woody and comedy, assuring me that since I had so much material already, it should take only eight or nine months. That was two years ago.

Since then I have gone with or followed Woody from New York to San Francisco to New York to Los Angeles to New York to Las Vegas to San Francisco to New York to Tarrytown to Los Angeles to Denver to Boulder to Los Angeles to Monterey to Los Angeles to New York to New Orleans to New York to Paris. I have sat and talked with him in hotel coffee shops and backstage dressing rooms and Rocky Mountain meadows; in his apartment, Madison Square Garden, and airplanes; on sound stages, Fifth Avenue, and the telephone. I have talked with him in movie theaters, in offices, and in my sleep, and what he has had to say was recorded on hours of tapes or carefully in a notebook, and when he is quoted it is accurate and in context. He has been helpful, courteous, and thoughtful throughout and he has been generous with both his time and his material, some of which has not been published before. I thank him.

I thank Jack Rollins and Charles H. Joffe for numerous kindnesses and Jack Grossberg for countless lunches. Larry Gelbart furnished me with a great deal of material and gave me considerable insight into comedy writing, and I appreciate his doing it.

The MacDowell Colony gave me several months of space, food, and quiet, and a bed to sleep it all off in, and they did it for free because I had no money to pay them. Anyone with an extra dollar or more who would like to help this worthy haven for painters, composers, and writers with a tax-free donation should contact Conrad Spohnholz, the director of the MacDowell Colony, Peterborough, New Hampshire 03458.

Carol Eisen Rinzler, who is occasionally mistaken for Romy Schneider, edited this manuscript with magic, and James O'Shea Wade came in for a perfect inning of relief. I am grateful and relieved.

Dorrie Lax and Lauriston L. Scaife would have liked to read this book, and Charles Brownell and Benjamin Curtis someday will.

Robert Rice and John Cushman have shown the faith of saints and angels, and Dorothy Pittman, Kathryn Lomax,

234

and Irena Wozniak of John Cushman Associates have been a divine chorus.

Custom requires that Oscar winners and writers of first books list 35 friends without whom they would surely still be mired in walk-on parts or in the goo of Chapter Three. Turns out custom has its reasons. So for cheering me on and cheering me up and helping me out I thank Tina Branch, David and Marilyn Brownell, Terry Clancy and Maureen Murphy, Bob and Sue Curtis, Joan Downs, Stephen and June Golden, Cynthia Scaife Gordon, Edward Hamilton and Terry Strauss, Barbara Hulsart, Jeannie Hutchins, Penelope Jessop, Jeremy and Elaine Kagan, John LaHoud, Maureen Orth, Peggy Owens Kuises, Bonnie Posmantur, Mark and Rhoda Clary Siegel, Edie Sparago, Alan Swyer and Ronnie Kern, Isabella King Watts, Philip White, Sharon and David Wilson, David and Jamie Rosenthal Wolf. And Clare Tweedy.

Peter Tauber keeps getting to heaven before I do, but he keeps drilling holes and pulling me through. In many ways he was the catalyst for this book. His help has been valuable, his friendship is priceless (but make an offer anyway and we'll talk). His new novel, *The Last Best Hope*, will soon be published. Buy it, if you will, and thank you for reading this.

Eric Lax
Paris
October, 1974

Index

237

238

239

240

Nichols, Mike, 4, 14, 22, 38, 75
Nietzsche, Friedrich, 37
Night at the Opera, A (movie), 89, 172, 176
Nixon, Richard, 201, 202–6
Notorious Landlady, The (movie), 187

On the Waterfront (movie), 169
Open City (movie), 74
O'Toole, Peter, 57, 58, 59, 60, 61, 62

Paar, Jack, 42
Paige, Janis, 188
Paleface (movie), 175
Palomar Pictures, 65
Panama, Norman, 182
Parents' Magazine, 67
Paths of Glory (movie), 198
Paulsen, Pat, 201
Peckinpah, Sam, 96
Penn, Arthur, 71, 168
Perelman, S. J., 23, 24, 40, 50, 174, 220, 221–23, 228
Picker, David, 84–85
Pinocchio (movie), 141
Place in the Sun, A (movie), 26
Plato, 38
Play It Again, Sam: movie, 3, 5, 20, 65, 68–69, 75–77, 94, 147, 174, 175, 212, 218; play, 75–77, 175, 209, 212, 213, 214–19
"P.M. East" (TV show), 199
Polanski, Roman, 96
"Politics of Woody Allen" (TV special), 100, 201–7
Porter, Cole, 41
Porter, Katherine Anne, 54
Portnoy's Complaint (book), 228
Potemkin (movie), 72
Prager, Stanley, 126, 211, 212
Prentiss, Paula, 57, 59, 74
Preservation Hall Jazz Band, 69, 133–39

Pride and Prejudice (play), 210
Producers, The (movie), 100, 126
Public Broadcasting System special, 100, 201–7
Pygmalion (play), 72

Ramon, Phil, 137
Randall, Tony, 188
Rice, Robert, 17
Rickles, Don, 16
Rittman, William, 218
Roberts, Ken, 43
Roberts, Tony, 212, 216, 218, 228
Robinson, "Big Jim," 134–35, 139
Robinson, Sugar Ray, 33, 222
Rollins, Jack, 22, 35, 38–40, 43, 52, 84, 98, 106, 130, 170, 213
Rose, Mickey, 29, 114, 116, 172, 213, 220
Rosen, Harlene, 34, 36, 37, 38, 43
Rosenbloom, Stuart, 96
Rosenblum, Ralph, 125–29, 130, 140, 144–45
Russell, Bertrand, 231

Sahl, Mort, 13–19, 22, 23, 38, 42, 116–17, 231
"Sanford and Son" (TV show), 186
Sayles, Emanuel, 135
Schneider, Romy, 57, 59, 61
Scholastic Magazine, 67
School for Scandal (play), 72
Scott, George C., 82
Second City players, 14
Sellers, Peter, 54, 57, 59, 60, 61, 62
Seven Year Itch, The (movie), 53, 209
Seventeen (magazine), 67
Seventh Seal, The (movie), 72, 167, 225
Sex (play), 219
Shaft (movie), 138
Shanker, Albert, 90
Shaw, Sam, 52, 54

241

242

About the Author

Eric Lax was born in British Columbia in 1944 and grew up in San Diego. Following graduation from Hobart College he spent two years on Tsis Island (pop. 185), Truk, Caroline Islands, as a Peace Corps Volunteer and then worked on the Washington Peace Corps staff in a variety of capacities. He retired from the government in 1970, went skiing for several months, and eventually became a free-lance writer. His articles have appeared in a number of newspapers and magazines, some of which still exist. He lives in New York City and South Starksboro, Vermont. *On Being Funny* is his first book.